Simply Sensational Decorating Projects

Simply Sensational Decorating Projects

Stevie Henderson
& Mark Baldwin

LARK BOOKS

A Division of
Sterling Publishing Co., Inc.
New York

JANE LAFERLA
editor

CHRIS BRYANT
art director

EVAN BRACKEN
photography

HANNES CHAREN
illustrations

10 9 8 7 6 5 4 3 2 1

Published by Lark Books, a division of
Sterling Publishing Co., Inc.
387 Park Avenue South, New York, N.Y. 10016

First Paperback Edition 2002
© 2001, Stevie Henderson and Mark Baldwin

Distributed in Canada by Sterling Publishing,
c/o Canadian Manda Group, One Atlantic Ave., Suite 105
Toronto, Ontario, Canada M6K 3E7

Distributed in the U.K. by:
Guild of Master Craftsman Publications Ltd.
Castle Place, 166 High Street, Lewes East Sussex, England BN7 1XU
Tel: (+ 44) 1273 477374, Fax: (+ 44) 1273 478606,
Email: pubs@thegmcgroup.com, Web: www.gmcpublications.com

Distributed in Australia by Capricorn Link (Australia) Pty Ltd.
P.O. Box 704, Windsor, NSW 2756 Australia

If you have questions or comments about this book, please contact:
Lark Books
67 Broadway
Asheville, NC 28801
(828) 253-0467

Printed in China.

This book was originally published as *Easy Style Room by Room: 50 Simple
and Sensational Projects for Home Decorating.*

ISBN 1-57990-308-8

CONTENTS

INTRODUCTION

FAST, EASY, AND TERRIFIC

When it comes to decorating your home, do you believe it costs a small fortune to get the look you want? That only a professional decorator can get the job done? That you need to throw everything away and start from scratch? If you're holding on to these basic misconceptions, you're holding yourself back from creating the beautiful interiors you admire. And, if you believe you can't do it yourself, we're here to tell you that it's simply not true.

This book contains projects that are quick and easy to make for every room in the house. For a fraction of the cost, not to mention hassle, *you* can transform your own home. Using fabric, paint, and wallpaper, you can have the rooms you envision, complete with that special window treatment, a custom fabric-covered table, and a room full of decorator pillows.

We have specifically avoided using any advanced techniques and specialized tools—most projects require only a glue gun, scissors, and staple gun. A few projects involve assembling pieces of stock lumber that are readily available from home improvement stores and lumber yards. Many of the projects call for recycling what you already have—chairs, lamps, or tables—or for transforming an inexpensive, flea-market find.

If you don't sew, don't worry! We've designed the fabric projects using the principles of anyone-can-do-it, no-sew decorating. Working with fabric is as easy as making hems with iron-on seam tape, and gluing or stapling pieces in place. You'll even find simple reupholstering that produces great (and almost instant) results. Only one project requires a sewing machine, and that uses a simple straight stitch.

HOW TO USE THIS BOOK

If you've hesitated tackling do-it-yourself home decorating, thinking it either too complicated or too time-intensive, this is the book for you. If you can measure accurately, use an iron, wield a hot glue and staple gun, hammer a nail, or use a drill, you have all the major skills required to make any project in this book.

The Tips and Techniques section gives you an overview of tools and materials, including how to select lumber and how to choose the correct weight of fabric for your project. Each project has its own complete tools and materials list so you can easily gather all that you need beforehand.

Step-by-step instructions lead you through the projects. More than 60 illustrations act as aides to help you visualize steps as you work. Most projects involve simple, straight measurements, making it easy to change a dimension here or there to suit your space requirements.

While we've assigned each project to a specific room, feel free to mix and match projects anywhere in the house. With an almost infinite palette of colors and fabrics available to you, you can have fun customizing projects to your taste and color scheme. So get ready to reap the satisfaction (and compliments) of knowing you've transformed your home room by room.

TIPS AND TECHNIQUES

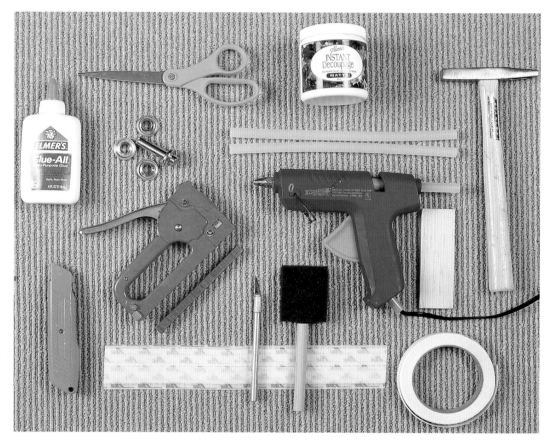

A few simple tools and materials are all you need.

CLOCKWISE FROM TOP: Scissors, decoupage medium, upholstery hammer, glue sticks, glue gun, wood, masking tape, hook-and-loop tape, disposable brush, craft knife, utility knife, staple gun, grommets, and glue.

TOOLS

The projects in this book require some basic tools. If you don't already own them, they will make useful additions to your household. All tools are readily available at general-merchandise and home-improvement stores. To determine which tools you will need for each project, simply read the instructions before beginning. We recommend that you gather all tools and materials before starting a project. That way, everything will be on hand, saving you both the time and added frustration of searching for missing items.

WORK SURFACE

No matter what kind of project you are making, a clean, flat work surface is important. You don't need a specially made professional surface. It can be as simple as a cleared kitchen counter or a dining table. Remember, if you're using a surface that serves multi purposes in your household, make sure you protect it properly before starting your project. Padding a surface with old cardboard and newspapers, then covering it with a plastic drop cloth will prevent damage to the surface as well as to the project.

STAPLES AND STAPLE GUNS

Staples are most often used in the projects for attaching fabric to wood. If you don't own a staple gun, a nominal investment will purchase this handy piece of equipment. You'll find you will use it many times over for projects and repairs around the house. Staple guns are available in many sizes and prices. Although electric models are available and nice to have if you are an avid crafter, a heavy-duty, manual staple gun will probably be all that you will need. The projects in this book were all completed using ⅜-inch-long (.9 cm) staples. You may find it worthwhile to purchase staples in a variety of lengths to accommodate the different thickness of material you may encounter in future projects.

SCISSORS AND ROTARY CUTTERS

If you have a pair of household scissors that you use for cutting paper, cardboard, and twine, you will want to purchase scissors that you can use exclusively for cutting fabric. Fabric scissors need to be sharp to cut the fabric smoothly and easily. Using them to cut anything other than fabric will dull the blades, making cutting fabric a tedious and frustrating experience. If you have school-age children, you may want to hide your fabric scissors for safe keeping from assorted club and school projects. If you want to save more time, you may wish to purchase a rotary cutter. However, you will need to purchase and use the special cutting pad as well. If you also sew or quilt, a rotary cutter would be a welcome addition to your equipment.

GLUE GUN

If you don't own a glue gun, we suggest that you immediately add one to your toolbox! They are a real timesaver, and are available in many sizes and prices. We suggest that you buy a fairly substantial glue gun. We also prefer to use the long glue sticks rather than the short ones, since frequent reloading becomes frustrating when you are working on large projects.

Hot glue can be used for many different applications. The glue comes in the form of solid sticks that you insert into the gun. The gun heats the glue stick, dispensing melted glue when you pull the trigger. For the projects in this book, hot glue is most often used as a substitute for hand stitching.

A word of extreme caution—use great care when working with a glue gun. The glue is incredibly hot when it is comes from the gun, and will blister your fingers instantly if you touch it before it cools. Never allow young children to use a glue gun, or allow school-age children to use a glue gun without adult supervision. Only work on a protected work surface when using hot glue.

HAMMER

When choosing a hammer, try it out before you buy it. Simply go to a hardware, general-merchandise, or home-improvement store, and lift the hammer you select several times before you decide that it is the one for you. Much like a golf club or a tennis racquet, a hammer works best when matched to the person who will be using it. While it's true that a larger hammer will drive the nail into the wood faster, a small person may be able to swing a larger hammer only once or twice before becoming exhausted.

MEASURING DEVICES

For most of the projects in this book you will need some kind of measuring device. For fabric, the tool of choice is an ordinary dressmaker's measuring tape. If you are planning to measure wood, however, a wide, steel tape measure is a good choice. A narrow tape bends more easily along the length of a board, making the measurement less accurate; and accuracy is paramount when cutting wood. Whenever you are cutting wood, use the same measuring device throughout the process, since two different devices can give slightly different measurements.

STRAIGHTEDGE

A metal straightedge is a versatile crafting tool both for measuring and to use as a guide when cutting with a utility knife. An ordinary steel ruler, 12 to 24 inches (30 to 60 cm) long, is sufficient.

T-SQUARE OR L-SQUARE

The most commonly used square is the framing square (or carpenter's square). A metal square can also be used to guide a utility knife, as well as marking a cut on a piece of wood and checking for right angles.

LEVEL

If you don't own a level, we suggest that you purchase one. You will use it for mounting brackets or hanging shelves and valances. A level that is either 2- or 3-feet (30 or 91 cm) long is sufficient for most home projects.

CHOOSING WOOD

In this book we have specified pine, which is the cheapest dimensional lumber in our part of the country. Feel free to substitute any softwood that is available where you live. You should inspect each and every board for defects and imperfections. Some stores or lumberyards will not allow you to hand-select individual boards. If this is the case, take your business elsewhere. You do not want to buy wood sight-unseen that might prove to be unusable afterward.

Examine the board for warping, cupping, and twisting. Warping is a curve along the length of the board, while cupping occurs across the width of the board. Twisting refers to its name, and will be obvious as you inspect the board. A good method to check for warping or cupping before you buy is to place one end of the board on the floor and look down its length. Then turn the board and look down the edge. Your own eye is the best test.

FABRIC

For each project, we have specified the weight of fabric you need to use. If you wish to substitute another fabric, choose weights and finishes that are similar to those specified. A project that specifies the use of a heavy-duty upholstery fabric will not turn out well if executed with a lightweight gauze-like material, and vice versa.

Fabric color is always optional, based on your personal taste and color schemes. Bear in mind that solids are almost always easier to work with than are patterns, and small patterns are easier to work with than large ones.

DROP

Every fabric pattern has a repeat. The length of that repeat is called a "drop". On a very small pattern, the drop may only be a few inches, but on a large-scale pattern, it may be measured in feet. When purchasing material, pay special attention to the pattern repeat as it relates to the finished look of the project. For example, if you are making a dust ruffle, you will want the same portion of the pattern to appear across the entire dust ruffle. This most likely means (unless you are uniquely lucky) that part of the fabric will be waste. For example, if your fabric has a 24-inch (60 cm) drop and you need 26 inches (66 cm) for your project, then 22 inches (56 cm) of the next repeat will be waste.

PLANNING FOR PATTERN

You will need to allow extra fabric for pattern placement on the project. For example, if you are covering a chair with a large-scale print, you want to be able to center the most attractive part of the print on the cushion and on the chair back. If you are in doubt about how much fabric to purchase, consult with the fabric-store personnel. We have found that most are very knowledgeable and very helpful.

ALWAYS BUY MORE

Unless you have chosen a very expensive fabric for your project, it always makes sense to slightly overbuy your materials. That way, if something doesn't work exactly as planned, you have extra fabric on hand. Remember, returning to the store for just one more yard (.9 m) is frustrating and time consuming. And, there's nothing worse than returning for more fabric and finding that the entire bolt has been sold.

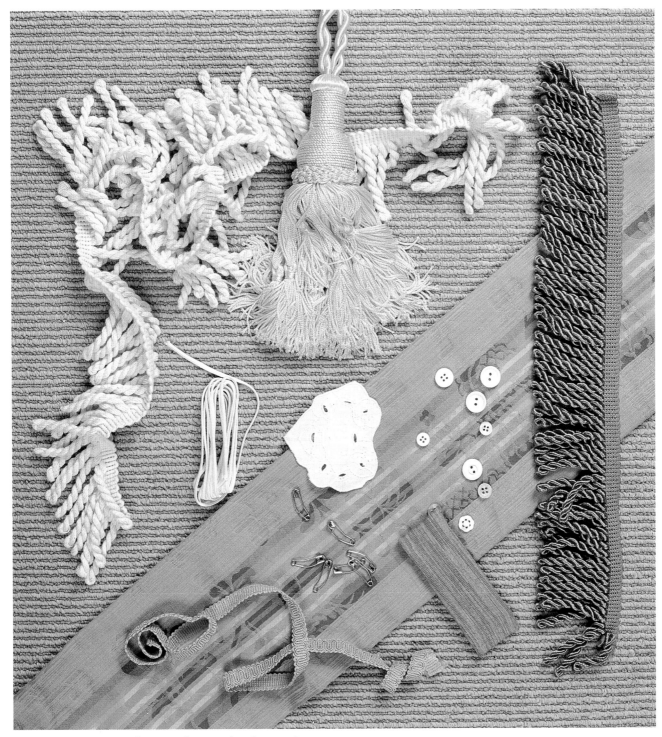

Keeping an assortment of trims and notions handy can enhance your projects. Clockwise from top: Tassel, bullion fringe, buttons, braids, safety pins, lace appliqué, cording, and fringe.

LIVING ROOM

Whether it's formal, or casual and comfortable, your living room is the focal point of your home. Because we actually like living in our living room, but also fancy a touch of elegance, we've used fabrics that are a bit more formal. Beyond the look of the room, we've tried to create an atmosphere that extends a welcoming invitation for lively conversations with friends, for special family gatherings, or for relaxing evenings at home.

SOFA SKIRT

Here's a little trick to turn a contemporary sofa into a gentler-looking piece of furniture. Adding the coordinating fabric skirt will tie it into the other fabrics in the room.

MATERIALS

Fabric that coordinates
with your sofa

TOOLS

Measuring tape

Scissors

Flat work surface

Glue gun and glue sticks

INSTRUCTIONS

Determining the Amount of Fabric

Each 54-inch width (1.37 m) of fabric will cover approximately 34 inches (.85 m) when gathered as shown in the photograph. Measure your sofa to determine the number of widths you will need. The length of each width is determined by the height of your sofa measured from the floor to the bottom of the cushions. For the skirt, measure from the floor to the bottom of the cushions, double that measurement, then add 8 inches (20 cm). We attached our skirt directly to the couch (underneath the pillows), using a glue gun. If you prefer, you can attach the skirt to a separate piece of fabric cut to the size of the couch underneath the pillows. If you do this, you may want to use a plain fabric, such as muslin, for this separate piece.

Making the Skirt

1 Cut a skirt panel from your chosen fabric to the measurements determined by your sofa.

2 Use iron-on seam tape to make a 1-inch (2.5 cm) hem along the two selvage edges of the skirt panel.

3 Fold the hemmed panel lengthwise, wrong sides together.

4 Lay the folded panel on a flat work surface. Keeping them together, gently gather the two top raw edges of the panel with your hands, until the panel width measures approximately 34 inches (.85 m) across the top. Secure the gathers, using hot glue.

5 Place one panel at one side of the sofa, under the cushion. Adjust the length as necessary so that the panel touches the floor. Glue the gathered edge of the panel to either the sofa or to the separate piece of fabric under the cushions. Continue adding panels, overlapping them slightly, until the sofa skirt is complete.

COCKTAIL TABLE COVER

Do you have a table destined for the trash? Remember, slip covers aren't just for chairs and sofas. With some fabric and cording, you can create an elegant accessory for any room.

MATERIALS

Craft paper

Old table*

54-inch-wide (1.37 m) fabric—to determine out how much you'll need, see *Making the Pattern* below

4 yards (3.7 m) of satin cording to coordinate with your fabric

Iron-on seam tape

TOOLS

Pencil

Scissors

T-square or framing square

Flat work surface

Straight pins

Iron and ironing board

Glue gun and glue sticks

Unless you want to seam two widths of fabric together, you are limited in the size table you can cover with 54-inch-wide (1.37 m) fabric. Measure your table first from the front, starting at the floor, then over the top of the table, and down the back to the floor again. Then measure it again from the side, starting at the floor, then over the top, and back down to the floor again. If one of these measurements is 53 inches (1.32 m) or less, you can cover the table using 54-inch-wide (1.37 m) fabric.

INSTRUCTIONS

Making the Pattern

1 To make this project, you need to make a paper pattern for the top, sides, front, and back of your table. To make certain all your corners are square, use a T-square or framing square. Measure the depth and width of your tabletop. Cut a paper pattern to these measurements, labeling it "top".

2 Measure the height of your table, then add ½ inch (1.3 cm) to that measurement. Measure the depth of your table, then add 1 inch (2.5 cm) to that measurement. Cut two paper patterns to these measurements, labeling each of them "side".

3 Next, measure the width of your table across the front, then add 1 inch (2.5 cm) to that measurement. Use the measurement for the height determined in step 2 (remembering to add the ½ inch [1.3 cm]). Cut two paper patterns to these measurements, labeling one of them "front" and one of them "back".

4 Arrange all five pattern pieces into a cross with the "top" piece at the center, one "side" on each side, the "front" at the bottom, and the "back" at the top. Tape them together to form one whole pattern. Measure the size of the pattern, and you will know how much fabric to buy.

Making the Table Cover

1 Place the entire pattern on your fabric, pin it in place, and cut it out.

2 Remove the paper pattern from the fabric. Use iron-on seam tape to make a ½-inch (1.3 cm) hem around the entire perimeter of the fabric. Clip the inside corners to keep the hems flat. Place the table cover over your table.

3 Cut a length of satin cord 1 yard (.9 m) long. Tie knots at each end, and then tie the length of cord in a bow. Use a glue gun to attach the cord bow to one top corner of the table cover. Repeat three more times, to cut, tie, and attach bows to each of the three remaining corners.

UPHOLSTERED CHAIR

Though the traditional styling of this chair makes it a classic accessory for any room, you can suddenly find yourself with a mismatched chair when you redecorate. With new upholstery, you can give a chair an instant facelift to change its look in no time.

INSTRUCTIONS

Surveying the Project

To upholster a piece of furniture, you must logically think through the project before you begin. The previous upholstery job will provide a starting place. Inspect the corners or other tricky areas to determine how they were folded or pleated. Also take note of any "dips" or "swaybacks" in the chair, and fill these depressions as needed as you work, with quilt batting. Don't be intimidated by the process. If you work slowly and thoughtfully, you'll be proud of your finished job.

Covering the Chair

1 Cut a piece of fabric large enough to cover each area, adding a 3-inch-(7.5 cm) allowance on all sides. We cut three pieces—one for the rear of the chair back, one for the face of the chair back, and one for the seat.

2 If needed, add quilt batting to each area to fill in any depressions.

3 Center the fabric over the area you are covering. Hold the fabric in place temporarily with straight pins.

4 Begin stapling the fabric to the chair frame, using enough staples to hold the fabric evenly and securely in place. As you work, use the scissors to trim the fabric just outside the staples. Since you will be covering the staples with the upholstery braid, try to keep the staples in a fairly uniform line. You can minimize the number of wrinkles if you start by stapling the center of one side, then the center of the opposite side. Then work your way out toward the corners, smoothing the fabric as you go. Next, staple the center of each of the remaining sides, and again work your way out toward the corners. Ease the fabric over the corners, eliminating as many wrinkles as possible. Finish the corners in the same manner as the old upholstery. If your stapler is too large for some areas of the chair, use a glue gun and hot glue to secure the fabric.

5 Finish the job by gluing upholstery braid over the staples and raw edges of your fabric.

MATERIALS

Old chair

Enough 54-inch-wide (1.37 m) fabric to cover your particular chair

Upholstery braid—enough ½-inch (1.3 cm) braid to cover the raw edges of the fabric*

1 bag of quilt batting (if needed) to fill in any dips or depressions in the chair seat

TOOLS

Tape measure

Scissors

Straight pins

Staple gun and staples

Glue gun and glue sticks

*If you can easily remove the braid from the old chair, do so, then measure it to find out how much new braid to purchase. Otherwise, measure the area where you want the braid to determine how much you will need.

PUFFED DRAPES

You can create this elegant drape, using two coordinating fabrics and a few rubber bands. Since it requires no sewing, you can have a completed window treatment in a few hours.

MATERIALS

Wooden curtain rod—figure the length to the measured width of your window*

Two coordinating fabrics—see *Determining the Amount of Fabric below* **

Rubber bands, approximately 25 to 30

Pushpins or thumbtacks

Tissue paper (optional)

TOOLS

Measuring tape

Scissors

* Ours extends 6 inches (15 cm) beyond the window on each side.

** As shown, we chose a pale green solid and paired it with a muted dusty peach and green stripe.

NOTE: You can use one color of fabric. Simply use two lengths of the same fabric, using the following instructions.

INSTRUCTIONS

Determining the Amount of Fabric

NOTE: Measure each color of fabric separately.

The number of puffs you make is dependent upon the width of your window. Each puff, as shown, covers approximately 8 inches (20 cm) of width, and requires approximately 1 yard (.9 m) of fabric. To find the number of puffs you need, divide the length of your curtain rod by 8 inches (20 cm). Then figure the amount of fabric for the puffs. For example, if each puff requires 1 yard (.9 m) of fabric, and you need five puffs, you will need a total of 5 yards (4.6 m) of fabric. We alternated the puffs, making five puffs using the green and four puffs using the stripe. We suggest that when using two different fabrics, you begin and end your row of puffs with the same color.

To figure the total yardage for the side drapes, first measure from the floor to the top of the curtain rod. To that measurement add 12 inches (30 cm). Double that measurement to get the amount of fabric needed to make a drape on each side of the window. Add the drape measurement to the puff measurement, and you will have the total yardage necessary.

Making the Curtains

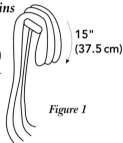

15"
(37.5 cm)

Figure 1

1 Allowing for a 12-inch (30 cm) end of fabric to puddle on the floor, bring the fabric up behind one end of the curtain rod. Double the fabric back over itself to form a 15-inch-deep (37.5 cm) puff, as shown in figure 1. Tie a rubber band around the puff to secure it.

2 Tuck any raw edges inside the puff, then spread the puff by pulling it across its width. Use thumbtacks or pushpins (on the back of the rod where they will not be seen) to secure the puff to the rod.

3 Repeat step 1 with the second color, placing the second puff next to the first one. If your fabric lacks enough body to hold the puff, you can crumple tissue paper and stuff it inside the puff.

4 Continue alternating the puffs, hiding the excess fabric behind the puffs, until you have covered the entire curtain rod.

5 Pull the remaining fabric to the backside of the rod, and let it puddle on the floor.

WINDOW SHADE

This roll-up fabric shade will provide privacy at night, and beautifully frame your window during the day.

INSTRUCTIONS

Determining the Amount of Materials

Since most windows are not entirely square, carefully measure the window for best results. To measure the length, measure from top to bottom in three places: left, center, and right. Use the shortest measurement of the three as your length. Next measure the width of the window at four or five different heights. Use the shortest measurement for your width.

Assuming that your window is 52 inches (130 cm) wide or less, you will need a piece of fabric 6 inches (15 cm) longer than the measurement of the length of your window, and 2 inches (5 cm) wider than the width of your window. If your window is more than 52 inches (130 cm) wide, you will need to seam additional lengths of fabric together.

You will also need lining fabric cut to the exact same size of the shade fabric. For the lining, we used plain off-white cotton. To make the ties for the shade, you will need four pieces of the shade fabric, each measuring 7 inches (17.5 cm) wide and 12 inches (30 cm) longer than the shade.

Making the Shade

1 Cut the shade fabric to the correct dimensions for your window, remembering to add 6 inches (15 cm) to the length and 2 inches (5 cm) to the width.

2 Place the fabric right side down on a flat work surface. Use iron-on seam tape to make a 1-inch (2.5 cm) hem along the bottom and sides of your fabric, as shown in figure 1. Repeat this step for hemming the lining fabric.

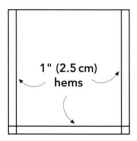

1 " (2.5 cm)
hems

Figure 1

3 Place the shade fabric right side down on the work surface. Center the lath over the bottom hem, and use a glue gun to attach the lath to the shade.

4 Place the lining wrong side down over the shade and attached lath, matching the hemmed edges on the sides and bottom. Use iron-on seam tape to join the lining to the shade on the two sides and the bottom.

Making the Ties

1 Cut four ties from the shade fabric, each measuring 7 inches (17.5 cm) wide and 12 inches (30 cm) longer than the shade.

2 Use iron-on seam tape to make a 1-inch (2.5 cm) hem in one end of each tie, as shown in figure 2.

1 " (2.5 cm)
hems

Figure 2

3 Use iron-on seam tape to make a 1-inch (2.5 cm) hem along one long edge of each tie.

4 Use an iron to press a 2-inch (5 cm) hem along the opposite long edge of each tie.

5 For each tie, fold the long hemmed edge over the pressed hem, overlapping the raw edge to form a 2½-inch-wide (6.25 cm) finished tie. Press in place. Use a glue gun to secure the hemmed edge along the entire length.

Completing the Shade

1 Lay the shade, lining side up, on a flat work surface. Smooth the two layers to eliminate any wrinkles. Place the 1 x 3 pine over the shade 4 inches (10 cm) from the top raw edges, as shown in figure 3.

MATERIALS

Two different fabrics, one for the shade, and one for the lining—see *Determining the Materials* below

1 piece of 1 x 3 pine, cut to the measurement of the width across the top of your window*

One piece of lath cut 1 inch (2.5 cm) shorter than the width of your window (lath cuts easily with a utility knife)

Iron-on seam tape

2½-inch (6.25 cm) finishing nails, 10

TOOLS

Scissors

Iron and ironing board

Large, flat work surface

Hammer

If you don't have the tools to cut the wood, most home centers or lumberyards will cut these to length for a nominal charge.

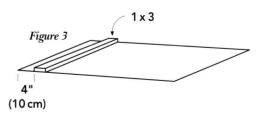

1 x 3

Figure 3

4"
(10 cm)

2 Wrap the raw edges of the shade and lining over the top of the board , and staple it securely to the edge of the board, as shown in figure 4.

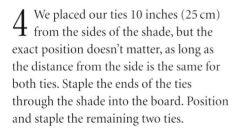

staples

Figure 4

3 The surface of the board that now faces your work surface will be placed against the top of the window during installation. You will attach the ties to this surface, allowing the ends of the ties to be hidden between the covered board and the top of the window. Place the shade on the edge of a kitchen counter or work table, so that the shade falls to the floor. Take two ties, and place the raw ends on one end of your shade, as shown in figure 5.

tie ends

shade

Figure 5

4 We placed our ties 10 inches (25 cm) from the sides of the shade, but the exact position doesn't matter, as long as the distance from the side is the same for both ties. Staple the ends of the ties through the shade into the board. Position and staple the remaining two ties.

5 You may want to enlist the aid of a helper to hang the shade. With the shade facing toward you, fit the lath inside the top of the window. Nail through the shade and the lath into the window frame, using 2½-inch (6.25 cm) finishing nails spaced approximately 6 inches (15 cm) apart.

FRINGED LAMP

We turned an old and ugly purple candlestick lamp into an elegant accessory with the addition of some gold paint and leftover bullion fringe.

INSTRUCTIONS

1 Working on old newspapers, use the gold paint and a small paint brush to paint the entire lamp base. We gave it two coats—the first coat is solid, and the second coat is heavy, dabbed-on spots of gold to give a mottled effect. Allow the paint to dry overnight.

2 Dribble gold paint randomly over the plain lampshade, allowing the paint to dry overnight.

3 Position the bottom of the fringe to almost cover the base of the lamp. Use hot glue to attach the woven end of the bullion fringe to the lamp.

4 Gluing as you work, gently wind the bullion fringe around the lamp, placing each layer of fringe a little higher than the previous layer. (You may want to wrap the lamp for practice before gluing.) When the base of the lamp is completely fringed, cut the glued fringe from the length of fringe, and hot glue the cut end to the previous layer.

5 We used the leftover fringe to make a finial for the top of the lamp. Simply wind up a length of fringe, then hot glue the end to keep it together. We tied a rubber band around the fringe to keep it upright. To cover the rubber band, we cut one single fringe, unwound it, and glued it over the rubber band.

MATERIALS

Old candlestick lamp

Small can of gold paint

1 yard (.9 m) of gold bullion fringe, in the length of your choice—ours measured approximately 3 inches (7.5 cm) wide

TOOLS

Old newspapers

Small paint brush

Glue gun and glue sticks

LAMPSHADE

Turn a plain white lampshade into a one-of-a-kind accessory. Pick your own favorite theme, add a little paint, and use an ordinary marker to create a shade that is uniquely yours.

MATERIALS

Plain white (or off-white) lampshade

Ordinary latex paint in your choice of colors—we used pale shades of peach, mauve, and green

Fine-lined permanent marker in a color to coordinate with your paints—we chose a dark green

TOOLS

Newspapers

Rags

Paint brush

INSTRUCTIONS

1 Dilute the paint with water until it is very runny. Spread old newspapers over your work surface to protect it. Dip the rag in the diluted paint, blot the rag to avoid any drips, then press the rag against the lampshade in random places. Allow the paint to dry.

2 Repeat step 1 two more times, using the second and third colors of paint, allowing the paint to dry between each coat.

3 Without diluting the paint, use one of the colors and a paint brush to drip the paint randomly over the lampshade. Allow the paint to dry overnight.

4 Decide on a theme for your lampshade— we chose "I love Florida" and compiled a list of things we love, such as: dolphins, sunglasses, palm trees, white sand, crystal water, etc. Your theme could be family, or summer, or your particular city.

5 Use the permanent marker and begin at the top of the lampshade by stating your theme. Keep writing your own list around the lampshade in a spiral, separating each item with three dots. Continue writing until you reach the bottom of the lampshade, and you're through!

TABLE SKIRT

Drape a round table with fabric, and you can immediately tie a room together. Using two different fabrics for this drape gives you more options for coordinating colors.

INSTRUCTIONS

Measuring the Table

The underskirt is simply two overlapping lengths of fabric draped over the table. To see how much fabric you will need, measure the table from the floor on one side, across the top, and down the other side to the floor. To that measurement, add 24 inches (61 cm) to allow the skirt to puddle on both sides.

Draping the Table

1 Cut two pieces of fabric to the length determined by your measurements above.

2 If you have access to a sewing machine, seam the two pieces together lengthwise, and press the seam open. If you don't sew the seam, simply press the selvage under on one long side of one piece of fabric.

3 Drape the unpressed length of fabric over the table so that the fabric puddles generously on the sides and back of the table. Don't worry about covering all of the table top. Drape the second length of fabric over the other side of the table, with the pressed edge overlapping the raw edge of the previous fabric. It should also puddle generously on the floor.

Making the Top Skirt

1 Use iron-on seam tape to make a 1-inch (2.5 cm) hem in all four edges of your 1½ yards (1.37 m) of coordinating fabric.

2 Center this hemmed square over the top of the two lengths of previously draped fabric, then cover the table with the fabric.

MATERIALS

Fabric for the underskirt—see *Measuring the Table* below

1½ yards (1.37m) of 54-inch-wide (1.37 m) coordinating fabric for the top skirt

Iron-on seam tape

Glass, cut to the diameter of the table top

TOOLS

Tape measure

Scissors

EASY SOFA TABLE

Here's a custom-covered sofa table you can make in just one afternoon. The base is made from three boards that you screw together, then you cover it with fabric. Our finished table as shown measures 36 inches (.9 m) wide and approximately 31 inches (.8 m) high.

MATERIALS

An 8-foot (2.4 m) length of 1 x 10 pine, cut in three pieces: one 36 inches long (.9 m) for the table top; and two, each 30 inches (76 cm) long for the table legs*

Four metal L-brackets, and enough ½-inch (1.3 cm) screws to attach them

1⅝-inch (4 cm) screws, 6

One piece of fabric measuring 99 by 22 inches (247.5 x 56 cm)

Iron-on seam tape

4 decorative brass corners (optional)

TOOLS

Screwdriver

Flat work surface

Scissors

Staple gun and staples

Glue gun and glue sticks

Hammer.

* If you can't cut the lumber your-self, most home centers and lumber-yards will cut it for a nominal charge.

INSTRUCTIONS

Constructing the Table

1 Place the 36-inch-long (.9 m) top over the ends of the two 30-inch-long (76 cm) legs as shown in figure 1. Screw through the ends of the top piece into the edges of the legs, using three evenly spaced 1⅝-inch (4 cm) screws.

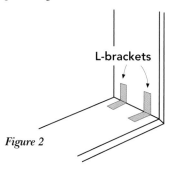

Figure 1

2 Place two L-brackets over one screwed joint, as shown in figure 2. Use the ¾-inch (1.9 cm) screws to attach the L-brackets to the top and leg.

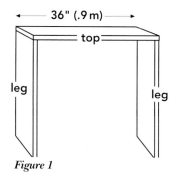

Figure 2

3 Repeat step 2 to attach the remaining two L-brackets to the opposite side of the table.

Covering the Table

1 Place the fabric right side down on a flat surface. Use iron-on seam tape to make a 1-inch-wide (2.5 cm) hem along one of the long edges of the fabric.

2 Center one leg of the U-shaped table on the fabric, placing the bottom of the leg ¾-inch (1.9 cm) from the edge of the fabric, as shown in figure 3.

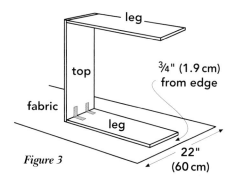

Figure 3

3 Beginning at the bottom of the table leg, wrap the long unhemmed edge of the fabric to the inside center of the table leg, then staple the fabric in place. Continue wrapping and stapling the fabric up the leg, across the underside of the table top, and down the inside of the opposite leg. Keep the fabric straight and smooth along the legs and top as you work—especially if you are using a plaid, striped, or geometric pattern.

4 Pull the opposite long hemmed edge over the stapled edge of the fabric and use a glue gun to hold the fabric in place. Begin working at the bottom of one leg, smoothing the fabric as you work.

5 To finish the bottom of the table legs, fold the fabric as if you were wrapping a package, then staple the fabric in place. Cut off any excess fabric to make the legs stand as flat as possible.

6 We nailed decorative brass corners to our finished table to add interest and to protect the fabric.

MASTER BEDROOM

The master bedroom, almost more than any room, needs to evoke feelings of peace and comfort. We think the luxurious bed drapes will not only surround you with your favorite colors, but with a sense of security and well-being— just the right combination for a good night's rest. The bank of pillows adds a designer's touch, while the pleated and appliquéd bench extends the color scheme into the room.

BED HANGINGS

With or without a four-poster bed, you can add a touch of romance to your bedroom using four pieces of floor-length fabric. We constructed the easy-to-make four-poster frame ourselves, but you can build a substitute canopy frame, using four curtain rods that you suspend from the ceiling.

INSTRUCTIONS

Making the Canopy

1 Working on a large, flat surface, lay out the curtain rods to the exact measurement of the length and width of your bed as shown in figure 1. Place the head and foot rods on top of the side rods. Five inches (12.7 cm) of the rods should extend beyond each of the four corners. Attach the finials. Using the plastic straps, secure the two rods at each of the four corners. Following figure 2, weave the straps around the rods in a figure-eight pattern, then pull the straps to secure them.

2 Using the drill and drill bit, pre-drill holes into the top rod at each corner, then insert a screw-hook in each of the holes.

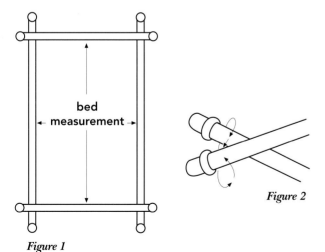

bed
← measurement →

Figure 2

Figure 1

MATERIALS

Four-poster bed

Or, if making your own canopy support…

4 curtain rods*

8 curtain-rod finials

4 long plastic straps—the ones used to hold bundles of electronic wires together; when you pull them tight, they will not release

Screw-in hooks, sturdy and preferably ½ inch (1.3 cm) longer than the diameter of one curtain rod

Ceiling hangers (with molly bolts)

Decorative metal chain, approximately 4 feet (1.2 m)

4 lengths of 54-inch-wide (1.37 m) lightweight fabric—to determine the amount of fabric you will need, see step 1 under Making the Hangings

1 yard (.9 m) of double-sided, adhesive-backed, hook-and-loop tape

4 yards (3.7 m) of coordinating ribbon (optional)

TOOLS

Drill and a drill bit slightly smaller than the diameter of the screw-in hooks

Scissors

Iron and ironing board

Glue gun and glue sticks

To determine the length of the curtain rods you will need, measure the length and width of your bed, then add 10 inches (25.4 cm) to each measurement. Purchase two curtain rods each in the length and width measurements.

3 Paint or stain the curtain rods (including the plastic straps) the color of your choice. If you wish to leave the rods their natural color, you may wish to tie some coordinating ribbons over the plastic straps to conceal them.

4 Insert the ceiling hangers above each of the four corners of your bed, matching the measurements of the curtain-rod canopy. Add lengths of decorative chain to the ceiling hangers. Hang the canopy by inserting the screw hooks in the canopy into the four chains. Note: If you have a tall ceiling, you may wish to add the fabric panels (see below) before hanging the canopy, then enlist the assistance of some willing helpers to aid you in hanging the draped canopy frame from the ceiling.

Making the Hangings

1 To determine the amount of fabric you will need for one hanging, measure from the top of the canopy support to the floor, then add 24 inches (61 cm) to that measurement. To get the total amount of fabric you will need, multiply this sum by six.

2 Cut six pieces of fabric, each measuring the measurement from the top of the canopy to the floor plus 24 (61 cm) inches.

3 Using an iron, press in a 1-inch (2.5 cm) hem along one of the long edges of each of the fabric panels. Use hot glue to keep the hems in place. Leave the other long edges unhemmed.

4 Gently fold (but do not press) each of the long lengths to the center of the fabric, overlapping the glued-hem edge over the raw edge as shown in figure 3. To hold the overlapped edges together, add a dab of hot glue approximately every 6 inches (15 cm).

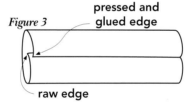

Figure 3

5 Working with the hemmed side up, gently gather one end of the fabric panel with your hands, until it measures just over 12 inches (30 cm) wide, as shown in figure 4. Press and pin the gathers in place.

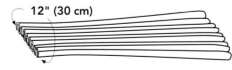

Figure 4

6 Cut a length of the double-sided hook-and-loop tape measuring 12 inches (30 cm) long. Do not separate the tape. Attach the sticky side of the tape to the seamed side of the gathered fabric panel, 6 inches (15 cm) from the raw edges as shown in figure 5. Remove the pins. Repeat on the remaining panels

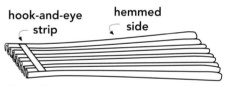

Figure 5

7 Wrap the panels around the curtain rod, as shown in figure 6. First, position the panels on the other side of the rod, with the hook-and-loop tape facing you. Bring the raw edges of the panels over the top of the curtain rod and then around, until the raw edges meet the tape. Then stick the raw edges to the tape.

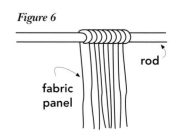

Figure 6

PLEATED AND APPLIQUÉD BENCH

Turn an old piano bench or garage-sale coffee table into an upholstered bedroom bench in an afternoon. The pleats are pinned, then stapled to the bench. A large motif on your coordinating print fabric becomes the appliqué, which you easily apply with fusible web.

MATERIALS

One piano bench or rectangular coffee table*

Quilt batting, enough to match the measurement of the top of your bench, plus a 3-inch (7.5 cm) allowance on all sides.

Two coordinating fabrics, each 54 inches (1.37 m) wide—see *Determining the Amount of Fabric* below**

1 large roll of iron-on seam tape

1 yard (.9 m) of fusible web

TOOLS

Measuring Tape

Scissors

Staple gun and staples

Iron

Ironing board or flat work surface

Straight pins

Glue gun and glue sticks

Craft knife (optional)

We used an old coffee table measuring 20 by 48 inches (50 x 122 cm). If you use a coffee table, it's best to find one with a top that only slightly overhangs the support structure. If the table you are using has a large overhang, you can cut off the excess.

** *Select a solid fabric and a coordinating fabric with a large motif. We used a large-scale floral. You will need more of the solid fabric.*

INSTRUCTIONS

Determining the Amount of Fabric

The top and pleated sides are made from the solid fabric. Since we wanted to eliminate sewing within the project, the method for making the pleats is based on purchasing a continuous length of fabric. If you have the option of sewing, you can purchase less fabric, then cut and sew the fabric together to make the length needed for your pleating.

Measure the width, length, and height of your bench or coffee table. As an example, the steps below use the measurements for the bench as shown. You will need to adjust the measurements and spacing of the pleats to accommodate your bench. For the top, the fabric needs to be as wide and long as the measurement for the top of your bench, plus a 3-inch (7.5 cm) allowance on all four sides, as shown in figure 1.

For the pleats, I spaced five, 11-inch-wide (27.5 cm) pleats 9¼ inches (23 cm) apart on the front and back of the bench skirt, and two on each side, giving me a total of 14 pleats. To get the total amount of fabric required for each pleat, I added 9¼ + 11 = 20¼ inches (23 + 27.5 = 50.5 cm). Since I had a total of 14 pleats, I needed 7.88 yards (7.2 m.) I rounded that to 8 yards (7.5 m) to provide a little

Figure 1

3" (7.5 cm) allowance, all sides

extra to fabric for overlapping the ends of the skirt at the back of the bench. If your bench is a different size, alter the spacing between the pleats, or change the number of pleats as needed.

Add the amount of fabric required for the top to the fabric needed for the pleats. I used a total of 9 yards (8.2 m) for this project. The height of our table is 17 inches (42.5 cm). Whatever your measurement, add 2 inches (5 cm) for the hem and 2 inches (5 cm) at the top. We cut our skirt fabric 21inches (53 cm) wide.

Covering the Top

1 Cut a piece of quilt batting to the dimensions of your top, adding a 3-inch-wide (7.5 cm) allowance on all four sides. Center the quilt batting over the top, and secure it to the table, using hot glue.

2 Cut a top from solid fabric to the dimensions of your top, adding a 3-inch-wide (7.5 cm) allowance on all four sides. Center the top over the quilt batting, then staple it to the sides of your bench. Use enough staples to hold the fabric evenly and securely in place. You can minimize wrinkling as you work by first stapling the center of one long side, then the center of the opposite long side. Next, work your way out toward the corners, smoothing the fabric as you go. Once the long sides are stapled, staple the center of each of the ends, and again work your way out to the corners. Finally, ease the fabric over the corners, eliminating as many wrinkles as possible.

Making the Skirt

1 From the solid fabric, cut a skirt to the dimensions required. Use iron-on seam tape to make a 1-inch-wide (5 cm) hem along one entire long edge, as in figure 2. Then use the iron to press in a 2-inch-wide (2.5 cm) hem along the opposite long edge.

Figure 2

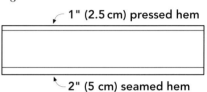

1" (2.5 cm) pressed hem

2" (5 cm) seamed hem

2 At this point, we suggest that you perform a preliminary fit. Using straight pins, temporarily pleat the top pressed edge. Then fit the pinned skirt around the bench, beginning at the center back of the bench. Make certain that the skirt is exactly the right length, that the pleats are even, that the center of a pleat falls at each of the four corners, and that the skirt overlaps slightly at the back of the skirt. Adjust the spacing or the width of the pleat if necessary. When the skirt fits perfectly, remove the skirt from the bench and press the pleats thoroughly, using a steam iron.

3 Replace the skirt on the bench, and temporarily hold it in place with straight pins. Beginning at the back of the bench, staple the skirt to the bench over the edges of the top. Place the staples fairly close together to prevent the skirt from sagging with time. Once stapled, remove the straight pins.

Making and Adding the Border

1 Cut the border from the coordinating fabric. Since you are using 54-inch wide (1.37 m) fabric, you will need to cut strips for piecing the border. Cut the strips across the width of the fabric, cutting one each for the front and back, and one each for both sides. Cut each strip approximately 5½ inches (13.8 cm) long.

2 Cut the side strips to the measurement of the sides plus 2 inches (5 cm). Cut the front and back strips to the front and back measurements plus 2 inches (5 cm). Use iron-on seam tape to make a 1-inch (2.5 cm) hem on each short end of the front and back border strips only, as shown in figure 3.

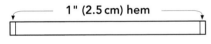

Figure 3

3 As shown in figure 4, use iron-on seam tape to make a 1-inch-wide (2.5 cm) hem along one long edge of all four border strips. Then use the iron to press in a 1½-inch-wide (3.8 cm) hem along the opposite long edges of the border strips.

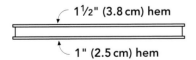

Figure 4

4 Fold the border strips with the 1-inch (2.5 cm) seamed hem over the 1½-inch (3.8 cm) pressed hem so that each border strip measures 2 inches (5 cm) wide, as shown in figure 5. Press in place.

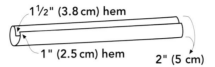

Figure 5

5 Cut a piece of quilt batting for each border strip. Each piece of batting should be as long as its border strip and 2 inches (5 cm) wide. Open each pressed border strip and insert the batting between the layers. Refold the layers, making sure that the 1-inch (2.5 cm) hem overlaps the 1½-inch (3.8 cm) hem. Using the glue gun, secure these long edges together.

6 Attach the border strips to the bench. First center the side strips on each side, wrapping the unhemmed edges to the front and back. Use the glue gun to attach the strips over the staples. Next, center the front and back strips, overlapping their hemmed side ends over the unhemmed side strips, then glue in place.

Making and Attaching the Bows

1 From the coordinating fabric, cut four lengths of fabric, each measuring 5½ by 47 inches (13.8 x 119.5 cm).

2 Use iron-on seam tape to make a 1-inch (2.5 cm) hem on each short end of the lengths of fabric. Then repeat steps 3 and 4 under *Adding the Border* to hem and fold each length.

3 Tie each of the lengths into a simple bow, taking care to keep the glued side toward the inside as you tie. Glue one bow to each of the four corners of the bench as shown in the photograph, covering the overlaps of the border strips.

Adding the Appliqué

1 Select the motif from the coordinated fabric that you wish to use as your appliqué, then cut out that section of the fabric. Don't try to cut out any details at this point.

2 Cut out a piece of fusible web that corresponds in size to the appliqué. Iron the web to the wrong side of the appliqué. At this point, do not remove the backing paper from the web.

3 Use scissors or a craft knife to cut out the pattern detail, cutting through the fabric, fusible web, and the paper backing.

4 Position the appliqué on the top of the bench. Remove the paper backing from web, and iron the appliqué to the top.

DECOUPAGED CLOSET DOORS

To add extra interest to otherwise plain white closet doors, we cut a floral motif from our wallpaper border, and decoupaged it to a door panel. It takes a little time to cut out the design, but the end result is well worth the effort.

MATERIALS

One roll of wallpaper border

Small jar of decoupage medium—available in art- and craft-supply stores

TOOLS

Small sharp scissors (manicure scissors work well)

Small paint brush

INSTRUCTIONS

Cutting the Design

1 Determine which portion of the border's design you wish to use. When choosing a motif from the overall design, make certain that it will look good by itself when you cut it out. Check that the portion of the design you select does not end with an incomplete motif, such as half a leaf.

2 Cut carefully around the design, using a pair of very small, sharp scissors. When cutting intricate designs, it is easier to hold the scissors steady and turn the paper while cutting. The edges of the design will also be more even if you use this technique.

3 Repeat step 2 to cut out as many additional designs as you will need. For our doors, we cut a total of four matching designs.

Adhering the Design

1 Brush a thin even layer of decoupage medium over the area where you intend to attach the design.

2 Brush a thin even layer of decoupage medium over the backside of the design you have cut out.

3 Carefully position the design over the area, and smooth it out carefully with your hands, beginning in the center and working out toward the edges. Use a soft cloth to eliminate any bubbles or wrinkles.

4 Brush another layer of decoupage medium over the design, again working from the center out toward the edges.

5 Repeat steps 1 through 4 for each of the remaining designs, making sure to position them in positions relative to the first one.

BOX-PLEATED DUST RUFFLE

If you've priced dust ruffles lately, even the plain white ones, you know they can be costly. Take heart! Then take up your iron and glue gun—this dust ruffle requires no sewing. You pleat panels of 54-inch-wide (1.37 m) fabric, selvage to selvage, before attaching them to the bed. For a small investment, it will look like you spent a fortune.

MATERIALS

54-inch-wide (1.37 m) fabric—
See *Determining the Amount of Fabric* below

Large roll of iron-on seam tape

TOOLS

Ruler or measuring tape

Scissors

Straight pins

Iron and ironing board

Glue gun and glue sticks

INSTRUCTIONS

Determining the Amount of Fabric

NOTE: We used a large floral pattern which requires more fabric than a solid, since the pattern needs to be matched across the ruffle. If you are not familiar with the term "drop," please read about it on page 10 of the *Tips and Techniques* chapter before beginning the project.

Measure the length and width of your bed. You will need enough finished pleated panels to cover one width and two lengths of your bed. To the total finished measurement you will also need to add 8 inches (20 cm), which is approximately enough fabric to allow your dust ruffle to gracefully round the corners at the head of the bed.

Since each of our finished panels measured 22 inches (56 cm), we divided the total measurement of the lengths and width (2 x length + 1 width + 8) by 22 inches (56 cm) to determine the number of panels we needed (plus factoring in the extra 8 inches [20 cm] mentioned above). Next, to get the measurement for the depth of your panel, measure the distance from the top of your box spring to the floor, then add 4 inches (10 cm). Depending on the "drop" of your fabric (see Note above), you may have to allow for additional material to match your fabric.

Making the Fabric Panels

1 From the fabric, cut one panel measuring 54 inches (1.37 m) by your depth measurement (the measurement from the top of your box spring plus 4 inches [10 cm]).

2 Use iron-on tape to make a 1-inch (2.5 cm) hem along the bottom edge of the fabric print, as shown in figure 1. (The bottom will be dependent upon the direction of the print.)

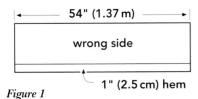

54" (1.37 m)

wrong side

1" (2.5 cm) hem

Figure 1

3 Use iron-on seam tape to make a 1-inch (2.5 cm) hem along the right side of the fabric panel, as shown in figure 2.

Figure 2

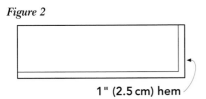

1" (2.5 cm) hem

4 Mark, then pin two 11-inch-wide (27.5 cm) pleats along the length of the fabric panel, leaving 16 inches (40.6 cm) between the two pleat folds, as shown in figure 3. You will have 15 inches (37.5 cm) of fabric remaining on the left side of the panel, which will be used for overlapping the finished panels.

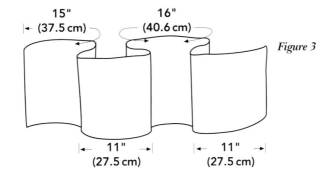

15" (37.5 cm)   16" (40.6 cm)

Figure 3

11" (27.5 cm)   11" (27.5 cm)

5 Using the iron, carefully press the two pleats into the fabric, then use a hot glue gun to secure them in place at the top of the panel.

6 Repeat steps 1 through 5 until you have enough panels (not counting the 15-inch-wide [37.5 cm] overlap) to equal two bed lengths, one bed width, plus 8 inches (20 cm).

Attaching the Fabric Panels

1 Remove the mattress. We attached our panels directly to the top of the box springs, using hot glue. However, if you wish to be able to remove your dust ruffle, you can attach the panels to an old sheet. Simply spread the sheet over the box spring, eliminating any wrinkles. Then trim the sheet so that it extends over the edge of the box spring approximately 2 inches (5 cm). Next, to prevent the sheet from moving, temporarily pin the sheet to the box spring, using straight pins. Then proceed with the next step.

2 Before actually gluing the pleated panels, you may wish to check the spacing by temporarily pinning the

panels in place around the bed, using straight pins. The dust ruffle will look more professional if one pleat ends at the corner of the bed, and the next pleat begins there. Begin at the head of the bed on the right side, and pin the first panel to the box springs (or sheet). Make certain that the fabric panel almost touches the floor, and that the pleats hang correctly. Raise the left side of the fabric panel just slightly, so that the overlapped fabric will not extend beyond the next panel at the floor.

3 Attach the second fabric panel so that the hemmed edge on the right side of the panel meets the pleated fold of the first panel, as shown in figure 4. Repeat until you have attached all the panels around the side, bottom, and opposite side of the bed.

4 When you are satisfied with the way the dust ruffle looks, attach the panels to the box spring (or sheet), removing the straight pins as you work.

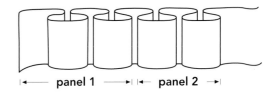

panel 1   panel 2

Figure 4

ROSETTE SWAG

If you can handle a rubber band and drive a nail, you can create and install these swags. The size of the rosettes can be adjusted to look terrific on any window. Pair the rosette swag with another length of fabric that drapes to the floor, and you have an elegant window treatment.

MATERIALS

54-inch-wide (1.37 m) fabric—
see *Determining the Amount of
Fabric* below

5 rubber bands

4 to 6 finishing nails

TOOLS

Flat work surface

Scissors

Hammer

INSTRUCTIONS

Determining the Amount of Fabric

To determine the amount of 54-inch-wide (1.37 m) fabric you need for one swag, first measure the width of your window. To that measurement, add 28 inches (71 cm), 14 inches (35.5 cm) for each of the rosettes. If you want to make the rosette swag with floor drape, first measure the length of your window, from the top to the floor, then add 24 inches (61 cm). To this measurement, add the measurement for one swag.

Making the Fabric Floor Drape

1 Cut a length of 54-inch-wide (1.37 m) fabric measuring 24 inches (61 cm) longer than the measurement from the top of your window to the floor.

2 Fold the long sides of the fabric drape to the center along its length, wrong sides together, as shown in figure 1. Tie a rubber band around one short end of the drape.

Figure 1

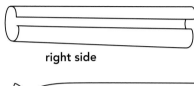

right side

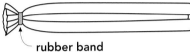

rubber band

3 Use a hammer and finishing nail to attach the drape just above the top corner of the window, nailing through the fabric just below the rubber band.

4 Fluff and adjust the drape so that it puddles on the floor and no raw edges are visible.

Making the Rosette Swag

1 Cut a swag panel from 54-inch-wide (1.37 cm) fabric measuring 28 inches (71 cm) longer than the width of the window.

2 Place the swag panel right side up on a flat work surface. Fold each of the long edges toward the center of the panel.

3 Gather one short end of the folded swag panel and tie a rubber band approximately 1 inch (2.5 cm) from the end, as shown in figure 2. Repeat on the opposite end of the panel.

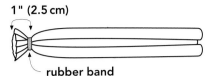

1" (2.5 cm)

rubber band

Figure 2

4 Turn the banded swag panel right side out, so that the rubber bands are now on the inside of the panel, as shown in figure 3.

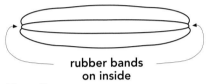

rubber bands on inside

Figure 3

5 Gather the panel approximately 12 inches (30 cm) from each end, and tie another rubber band around the panel at that point, as shown in figure 4.

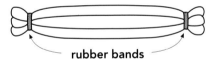

rubber bands

Figure 4

6 Working on one end, bring both of the rubber bands together, and flatten the surrounding fabric to form a rosette, as shown in figure 5. Repeat to form a rosette on the opposite end of the swag panel, taking care to match the size of your previous rosette.

Figure 5

7 Check the width between rosettes against the width of your window and adjust the rubber bands, if necessary.

8 Position one of the rosettes to cover the fabric drape attached to the window, and nail through the center of the rosette into the wall at the corners of the window. Repeat the procedure to attach the remaining rosette to the opposite side of the window, making sure that the rosettes are placed at the same height and distance from the corners of the windows. Adjust the fabric between the rosettes until it covers the window at the top and drapes gently at the bottom. If necessary, use additional nails to take up the slack at the top behind the rosettes.

MATERIALS

1 yard (.9 m) of fabric—we chose a large floral to coordinate with the rest of our room

1 round pillow form, 12 inches (30 cm) in diameter

1 appliqué that coordinates with your fabric, measuring approximately 3½ inches (8.8 cm) in diameter

TOOLS

Flat work surface

Scissors

Glue gun and glue sticks

PLEATED ROUND PILLOW

You can find many attractive ready-made trims to enhance any design. We had purchased the white embroidered appliqué for another project, then found it worked well with this pleated pillow.

INSTRUCTIONS

Covering the Pillow

1 Cut a 36-inch (.9 m) square from the fabric.

2 Place the fabric square right side down on a flat work surface, and center the pillow form on top of it.

3 Gently fold a small pleat of fabric over the outer edge of the pillow form, and pin it to the top center of the form, as shown in figure 1.

4 Continue folding small pleats to the center of the pillow form, working in sequence around the entire pillow. As you work, watch that the form does not slide off the center of the fabric. After every third pleat, trim off the excess fabric, then glue the pleat in place with hot glue. You want the joining at the center to be as flat as possible. As you work, eliminate as much of the excess fabric as you can, and keep the center joining neat.

5 Finish the pillow by gluing the appliqué over the center joining.

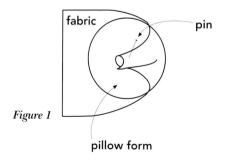

fabric　　　　　　　pin

Figure 1

pillow form

PUFF PILLOW

This pretty pillow is as easy to make as tying up your hair. With the addition of satin cording and a silk rose, it looks like an expensive accessory from an exclusive boutique.

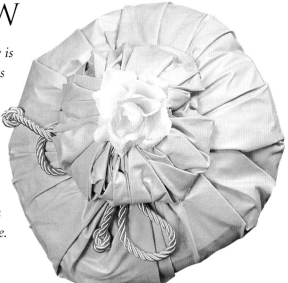

MATERIALS

1 yard (.9 m) of 54-inch-wide (1.37 m) lightweight reversible fabric*

1 round pillow form, 12 inches (30 cm) in diameter

1 heavy-duty rubber band

1 yard (.9 m) of satin cording

1 silk rose

TOOLS

Flat work surface

Scissors

Glue gun and glue sticks

*By reversible, we mean that the fabric looks the same on both sides.

INSTRUCTIONS

1 Place the fabric wrong side up on a flat work surface. Center the pillow form on the fabric, and gently pull the edges of the fabric over the center of the form. Secure the fabric at the center with a heavy-duty rubber band. Adjust the gathers until they are evenly spaced around the pillow.

2 Leave approximately 6 inches (15 cm) of fabric extending from the rubber band, using the scissors to cut off the excess fabric.

3 Tie the satin cord over the rubber band, ending in a large bow. Tie knots in the free ends of the cord.

4 Find the center of the gathered fabric and flatten it against the pillow. Fold the raw edges under, around the entire circle, then glue the folded edges to the pillow to form a smaller gathered circle.

5 Glue the silk rose in the center of the smaller gathered circle.

MATERIALS

54-inch-wide (1.3 m) fabric,
2 yards (1.8 m) in a color of
your choice, and ⅓ yard (.3 m)
of a coordinating fabric

1 standard pillow

Iron-on seam tape

TOOLS

Scissors

Iron

Ironing board

Glue gun and glue sticks

ANGEL-WING PILLOW

*Dare we say this pillow cover is "heavenly?" With a little sleight
of hand, and the addition of a rubber band, you create the wings.*

INSTRUCTIONS

Covering the Pillow

1 From the 2 yards (1.8 m) of fabric
cut one pillow cover measuring
60 by 48 inches (150 x 122 cm).

2 Use iron-on seam tape to make a
1-inch (2.5 cm) hem along one of
the 60-inch-long (150 cm) edges.

3 Place the fabric right side down
on a flat surface, with the
hemmed edge at the bottom. Center
the pillow over the fabric, then fold
the unhemmed edge to the middle of
the pillow. Fold the hemmed edge
over the unhemmed edge, and secure
it with hot glue.

4 Fold the two remaining edges to
the center, and secure them in
place with hot glue. (Don't be too
concerned about neatness, since the
joining of the two fabrics will be covered in a later step.)

Adding the "Wings"

1 Cut a fabric rectangle measuring
26 by 12 inches (66 x 30 cm) from
the ⅓ yard (.3 m) of fabric.

2 Use iron-on seam tape to make a
1-inch (2.5 cm) hem on all four
sides.

3 With its right side up, center the
rectangle (which will become the
"wings") lengthwise on the covered
pillow over the previously glued joint.
Bring the two ends together, then
loosely tie them together with a rubber band. Pull the two ends to the top
and bottom of the pillow so that the
rubber band is now behind the glued
joint. Spread out the "wings".

NECK-ROLL PILLOW

The satin cording on this pillow adds an elegant look. The rolled shape provides extra neck support when catching a nap.

MATERIALS

1 yard (.9 m) of lightweight fabric—we chose a large floral chintz

1 neck-roll pillow form (or old pillow)—the one shown is 16 inches (40 cm) long

2 yards (1.8 m) of satin cording that coordinates in color with the fabric

Iron-on seam tape

TOOLS

Scissors

Iron

Ironing board

Glue gun and glue sticks

INSTRUCTIONS

1 Measure the circumference and length of your pillow. Add 6 inches (15 cm) to the circumference and 16 inches (40 cm) to the length. Cut a piece of fabric to those dimensions.

2 Use iron-on seam tape to make a 1-inch (2.5 cm) hem along the two long edges of your fabric.

3 Use iron-on seam tape to make a 4-inch (10 cm) hem along the two short edges of your fabric.

4 Center the pillow form along one long edge of your fabric, and roll the fabric over the form. Secure the final edge with several dabs of hot glue.

5 On one side of the pillow, gather the fabric with your hands. Secure the gathers with a length of satin cording by wrapping the cording around the gathers close to the pillow end. Tie a bow in the cord, then tie knots in the ends of the cord, trimming any excess cording with scissors. Repeat on the other side of the pillow.

back of pillow

MASTER BATH

Pamper yourself! If you want to capture the essence of leisurely living, create this romantic and glamorous master bath. The upholstered chaise lounge provides a quite corner just for you, while the canopied dressing table provides a place to primp in movie-star splendor. From the window treatment to the vanity lamp, you will feel the quiet luxury of this great getaway that's only a few steps away.

UPHOLSTERED CHAISE LOUNGE

This old chaise lounge was destined for the landfill when we rescued it from the curb. With a little tender-loving care, it has a new life in our bathroom. We don't claim to be trained upholsterers, but as you can see, it is possible to redo a chaise yourself with great results.

INSTRUCTIONS

Surveying the Project

To upholster a piece of furniture, you must logically think through the project before you begin. The trick is to think in layers. The previous upholstery job will give you the answer. Survey your piece to determine how the previous upholstery was done. Also take note of any "dips" or "swaybacks" in the chair, and fill these depressions by adding quilt batting as needed as you work. Don't be intimidated by the process. If you work slowly and thoughtfully, you'll be proud of your finished job.

Covering the Arms and Back

1 To begin, remove the seat of the chaise and set it aside.

2 Normally the inside of the chaise arms are the first to be covered. Using the chaise as a pattern, cut a piece of fabric large enough to cover the inside of the arms and to wrap around to the underside of the arm, making sure that the fabric is oriented the proper direction. For example, if you are using a floral fabric, make sure that the flower is right-side-up

on the finished chaise. Allow an additional 2 to 3-inch (5 to 7.5 cm) allowance as a margin for error, and for attaching the fabric to the frame. Staple the fabric tightly to the frame at the bottom inside of the arm. Staple the center bottom of the fabric to the center of the frame, and then work out to the edges in both directions, easing the fabric around the front of the arm.

3 Next, bring the fabric over the arm, and staple it to the chaise frame under the arm, as shown in figure 1. Add quilt batting to the arm as necessary. Again begin stapling in the center of the underarm, and work out in both directions. Repeat steps 2 and 3 to cover the opposite chaise arm.

4 Cover the back of the chaise next, using the same procedure that you used to cover the chaise arms.

Covering the Underarms and Chair Back

1 This is the part where we recommend cutting a paper pattern. Pin a piece of craft paper to the underarm of the chaise, and cut it to fit properly, as shown in figure 2. It should cover

MATERIALS

Old chaise lounge

54-inch-wide (1.37 m) fabric, enough to cover your particular chaise—estimates range from 5 yards (4.5 m) for a small chaise to 6 yards (5.4 m) for a large one

2 or 3 bags of quilt batting

Large roll of iron-on seam tape

Upholstery trim, ½-inch (1.3 cm) braid

TOOLS

Ruler or tape measure

Scissors

Craft paper

Iron and ironing board

Straight pins

Staple gun and staples

Glue gun and glue sticks

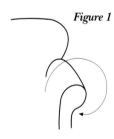

Figure 1

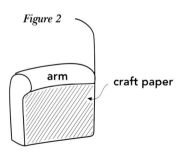

Figure 2

arm

craft paper

just the flat portion of the chair side, under the arm. When the pattern is perfect, remove it from the chair, and cut a piece of fabric to that size, adding a 2-inch (5 cm) allowance around the edges.

2 Use an iron to press a 2-inch (5 cm) hem along the top and front edges of your fabric piece, as shown in figure 3.

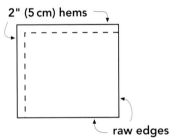

2" (5 cm) hems

raw edges

Figure 3

3 Place the hemmed fabric over the chair. Beginning at the corner of the seat front, staple through the pressed fabric hem into the chaise frame, covering the raw edges of the previous arm fabric under the chair arm. Smooth the fabric, and work to the back of the arm. Continue stapling down the front side of the arm. Don't worry about the staples showing, they will be covered by braid in a later step.

4 When the front and seat of the arm sides are complete, pull the raw edges to the back of the chair, and staple them in place, working from top to bottom, as shown in figure 4.

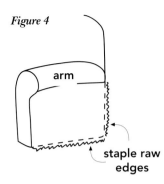

Figure 4

arm

staple raw edges

5 Next, staple across the bottom of the outside arm, beginning in the center and working out. Then repeat steps 2 through 5 to cover the opposite arm side.

6 Repeat the same steps to cover the chair back. The only difference is that you will press under both of the side allowances on the chair back, rather than just the front side.

Adding the Skirt

1 Measure the distance from the seat of the chaise (minus the seat which you have removed) to the floor, then add 4 inches (10 cm) to that measurement. That will be the length of the chaise skirt.

2 Next, measure entirely around the chaise, and multiply that number by 2. This will give you the total amount of fabric you will need for the skirt ruffle.

3 Cut enough fabric to the measurements determined in steps 1 and 2. If you have access to a sewing machine, seam the panels together to

form one length. If you don't have a machine, you will need to hem both sides of each panel. We made our skirt using a toile pattern, which needs to be matched across the ruffle, and requires more fabric than a solid. If you are not familiar with the term "drop", please read that section of the *Tips and Techniques* chapter on page 10 before cutting the panels.

4 Use iron-on seam tape to make a 2-inch (5 cm) hem along the bottom edge of the entire skirt.

5 If you are applying separate panels, use iron-on seam tape to make a ½-inch (1.3 cm) hem along both sides of each panel.

6 The next step is to attach the skirt to the chair frame. We recommend that you attach the skirt temporarily to the chaise, using straight pins. Using your hands, gather the seat fabric, then pin it in place all the way around the chaise, making sure that the hemmed edge of the skirt almost (but not quite) touches the floor and hangs straight.

7 When you are satisfied that the skirt is evenly gathered around the entire chaise, staple through the seat of the skirt into the chaise frame. Trim off any excess fabric above the staples. The front raw edges of the skirt will be covered by the chaise seat, and the raw edges around the back of the chaise will be covered with fabric trim.

Adding the Trim

1 Use a glue gun to glue upholstery braid over the exposed staples underneath the arms and on the back of the chaise.

2 To make the fabric trim to cover the skirt staples on the back of the chaise, first measure the total length required (from the front of one arm, around the back, and to the front of the opposite arm), then add 2 inches (5 cm) to that measurement.

3 Cut a 2½-inch-wide (6.25 cm) strip of fabric to the length determined in step 2. If your fabric is not wide enough to cut the entire length, cut three separate pieces: two for the sides, and one for the back.

4 Use iron-on seam tape to make a ½-inch (1.3 cm) hem in each short end of the trim.

5 Use iron-on seam tape to make a ½-inch (1.3 cm) hem along one long edge of the trim. Then use iron-on seam tape to make a 1-inch (2.5 cm) hem along the opposite long edge of the trim.

6 Fold the strip with the ½-inch (1.3 cm) seam over the 1-inch (2.5 cm) seam until the strip measures 1 inch wide (2.5 cm). Press in place.

7 Cut a piece of quilt batting measuring 1 inch (2.5 cm) wide and the length of the hemmed trim.

8 Open the pressed fabric strip and insert the quilt batting between the layers. Refold the layers, making sure that the ½-inch (1.3 cm) hem overlaps the 1-inch (2.5 cm) hem. Use a glue gun to secure the edges together.

9 Use a glue gun to attach the trim over the staples, beginning and ending at the front of the chaise.

Covering the Seat

1 Cut a piece of quilt batting to the dimensions of your seat, adding a 3-inch (7.5 cm) allowance on all four sides. Center the quilt batting over the seat, and temporarily secure it, using hot glue.

2 Cut a fabric seat, adding a 3-inch (7.5 cm) allowance on all four sides. Center the seat over the quilt batting, and staple it to the underside of your seat. Use enough staples to hold the fabric evenly and securely in place. You can minimize the number of wrinkles if you start by stapling the center of one long side , then the center of the opposite long side. Then work your way out toward the ends, smoothing the fabric as you go. Next, staple the center of each of the ends, and again work your way out toward the corners. Ease the fabric over the corners, eliminating as many wrinkles as possible.

3 Replace the completed seat on the chaise lounge.

CURTAIN ROOM DIVIDER

If you have a space that needs some additional privacy—or a spot that could look a bit cozier—here's the solution. Just add a length of fabric across the doorway, attach a tie-back and tassel, and you have instant ambiance.

MATERIALS

1 length of 105-inch-wide (2.6 m) sheer fabric—see step 1 to determine the length you will need*

1 decorative curtain tieback with tassel

2 x 4 pine board cut to the measured width across the top of your doorway

2½-inch-long (6.25 cm) finishing nails, approximately 5

1 cup hook

TOOLS

Measuring tape

Scissors

Staple gun and staples

Hammer

Paint and brush (optional)

We used a white dotted-Swiss.

INSTRUCTIONS

Making the Curtain

1 To determine the length of fabric you will need, measure from the top of your doorway to the floor, then add 3 yards (2.7 m) to that measurement. Our doorway measures 40 inches (1 m) across. If you have a wider doorway and want to extend the curtain all the way across, you can use more than one width of fabric for your project.

2 Cut a length of sheer fabric equal to the measurement from the top of the doorway to the floor plus 2½ yards (2.3 m). Save the remaining one-half yard (.45 m) of fabric for later use to make a ruffle at the top.

3 Cut the 2 x 4 just slightly shorter than the measured width across the top of your doorway. Note: If you don't want the wood grain to show through the sheers, you'll need to paint the wood the color of your fabric.

4 Staple the center of one raw edge of the fabric to the center of the cut board, placing the wrong side of the fabric against the board as shown in figure 1. Then staple the two selvage edges to the two ends of the board.

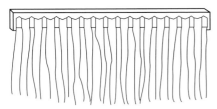

Figure 1

5 Gently gather the fabric onto the board between the center and the ends, adjusting the gathers with your hands until they are even and straight. Staple the gathers in place.

6 Hold both ends of the board in your hands with the staples on the top, and roll the board away from you until it is upside-down and you can no longer see the staples as shown in figure 2. Again, staple across the gathers over what is now the top of the board.

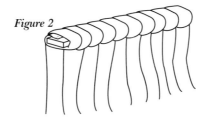

Figure 2

Finishing

1 Fold the remaining ½ yard (.45 m) of fabric in half lengthwise, with wrong sides together.

2 Gently gather the raw edges of the fabric and staple the gathers to the board, placing them over your previous staples, as shown in figure 3.

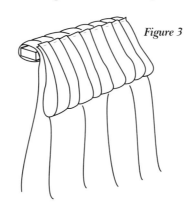

Figure 3

3 To attach the divider to the top of the doorway, simply nail through the top into the top of the doorway, using 2½-inch (6.25 cm) finishing nails. Gently pull the fabric over the nails until they are no longer visible.

4 Fit the curtain tie-back with attached tassel around the curtain and adjust the curtain until you are pleased with the drape. Install a cup hook on the door frame to hold the end of the tieback.

5 Fit the tieback over the hook to hide it, then readjust the drape, letting the remainder of the curtain puddle on the floor.

TASSELED CURTAINS

If you have always liked the look of tasseled tieback curtains, here's a new and different way to use them for decorating your window.

MATERIALS

54-inch-wide (1.37 m) medium-weight fabric—see *Determining the Amount of Fabric below**

Lightweight, sheer fabric—see *Determining the Amount of Fabric* below

Iron-on seam tape

Two tasseled curtain tiebacks—one for each width of your curtain

Small length of string

TOOLS

Measuring tape

Scissors

Glue gun and glue sticks

**We used a pale green and yellow toile.*

INSTRUCTIONS

Determining the Amount of Fabric

For the curtains, measure the height and width of your window. One length of 54-inch-wide (1.37 m) fabric will cover approximately 18 inches (45 cm). Since our window is 36 inches (.9 m) wide, we used two widths. The length of the fabric should be twice the height of the window plus 4 inches (10 cm).

To make the ruffle at the top, you will need a very lightweight sheer—as shown, our fabric was 105 inches (2.62 m) wide. For our 36-inch-wide (.9 m) window, we only needed one width that was cut 24 inches (61 cm) long.

Making the Curtain

1 Cut a 54-inch-wide (1.37 m) fabric panel to the proper length for your window. (Twice the height of the window plus 4 inches [10 cm].)

2 Use iron-on seam tape to make a ½-inch (1.3 cm) hem in both selvage sides of the panel, as shown in figure 1.

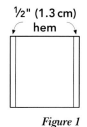

½" (1.3 cm) hem

Figure 1

3 Lay the panel right side down on a flat work surface, and fold it in half lengthwise by overlapping one 54-inch (1.37 m) edge over the other, as shown in figure 2. Use hot glue to secure the two ends together. Repeat the procedure for each fabric panel needed to cover the width of your window.

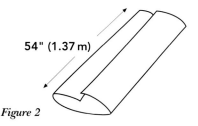

54" (1.37 m)

Figure 2

4 Insert a curtain rod through each of the fabric panels, adjusting the panels until the glued joint is at the top back of the curtain rod.

5 Add a curtain tieback to the center of each of the fabric panels, placing one side of the tieback on the front of the curtain and one side on the back. Using a small length of string, tie the two sides of the tieback together at the top. Adjust the tieback so the string is not visible on the front of the curtain.

6 Fold the 105-inch-wide (2.62 m) sheer fabric in half lengthwise, placing wrong sides together.

7 Lay the folded sheer panel on a flat work surface. Gently gather the two top raw edges of the panel with your hands, until the panel width measures approximately 36 inches (.9 m) across the top, keeping the raw edges straight and even. Secure the gathers, using hot glue. Note: Gather the fabric to the width of your window. If the window is less than 36 inches (.9 m) wide, you will have more gathers than shown; if the window is wider, you will have fewer gathers, or you can add an extra panel.

8 Place the gathered sheer panel over the top of the curtain and attach the raw edges of the panel to the glued seam in the curtain at the back.

DRESSING TABLE

With the addition of a fabric cover, we turned two purchased drawer units into this charming dressing table. Depending on the size of your room, you can easily purchase the size of unit you need to fit your space.

MATERIALS

2 purchased drawer units—ours measured 28 by 18 by 21 inches (71 x 45.5 x 53.5 cm)*

1 piece of ½-inch-thick (1.3 cm) plywood— we cut ours 38 by 22 inches (96.5 x 56 cm) to fit over the tops of both drawer units

2 pieces of quilt batting—see *Determining the Amount of Fabric* below

Print or solid 54-inch-wide (1.37 m) fabric for the front and side table drapes, and for covering the top of the dressing table and canopy— see *Determining the Amount of Fabric* below

4 metal brackets (optional)

3 pieces of wood lath, two pieces cut to the length of the plywood sides, and one piece cut to the length of the plywood front

1-inch (2.5 cm) finishing nails

Sheer, lightweight fabric for the canopy drape, 105 inches (2.62 m) wide— see *Determining the Amount of Fabric* below

Adhesive-backed hook-and-loop tape, one piece cut to the width of your finished dressing table top.

3 linear feet (.9 m) of 1 x 12 pine

2½-inch (6.25 cm) finishing nails

TOOLS

Scissors

Measuring tape

Glue gun and glue sticks

Staple gun and staples

*The ones we bought fit a variety of drawer sizes, allowing us to mix or match. If you don't need drawers, you could also use a small garage-sale table.

**If you're not handy with a saw, most home centers will be happy to cut the plywood to size for you for a nominal charge.

INSTRUCTIONS

Determining the Amount of Fabric

The quilt batting pads both the table top and canopy top. For the table top, you will need a piece of batting the size of your plywood top plus a 2-inch (5 cm) allowance on all four sides. For the canopy top, you will need a piece measuring 40 by 14 inches (101.5 x 35.5 cm).

To cover the top of our dressing table and the canopy top, and to make the front and side panels, we used a large floral print. For the table top, measure the width of the sides and front of your plywood top. You will need enough fabric to cover the top of the plywood, plus a 2-inch (5 cm) allowance on all four sides. For the canopy top, you will need a piece of the same fabric measuring 40 by 14 inches (101.5 x 35.5 cm).

We used two widths of the 54-inch-wide (1.37 m) fabric to drape the front of our dressing table, and one width of the same fabric to drape each of our sides. To determine the length of each drape, measure from the top of the plywood to the floor, then add 8 inches (20 cm) to that measurement.

We measured the distance from our ceiling to the floor, and added 1 yard (.9 m) to that measurement. Since the fabric was wide, we cut only one length to our measurement, then cut the fabric it in half lengthwise to give us two panels.

Covering the Top

1 Cut a piece of quilt batting to the dimensions of your plywood top, adding a 2-inch (5 cm) allowance on all four sides.

2 Center the quilt batting over the plywood top, and temporarily secure it to the wood, using hot glue.

3 Cut a piece of fabric to the dimensions of your top, adding a 2-inch (5 cm) allowance on all four sides.

4 Center the fabric over the quilt batting, and staple it to the underside of the plywood. Use enough staples to hold the fabric evenly and securely in place. You can minimize the number of wrinkles if you start by stapling the center of one long side, then the center of the opposite long side. Then work your way out toward the ends, smoothing the fabric as you go. Next, staple the center of each of the ends, and again work your way out toward the corners. Ease the fabric over the corners, eliminating as many wrinkles as possible.

5 Place the completed top over the drawer units. Since the units are heavy and stable, we did not fasten the top to them, but if you have small children, you may wish to attach brackets under the top to permanently attach it to the drawer units.

Adding the Side Drapes

1 Cut a piece of lath measuring the same length as the sides of the fabric-covered top.

2 Cut a piece of 54-inch-wide (1.37 cm) fabric the measurement from the top of the dressing table to the floor, plus 8 inches (20 cm).

3 Use iron-on seam tape to make a ½-inch (1.3 cm) hem along both

selvage edges and across the bottom of the fabric.

4 Staple the center of the unhemmed raw edge of the fabric to the center of the lath strip, placing the wrong side of the fabric against the lath, as shown in figure 1. Then staple the two ends to the two ends of the lath.

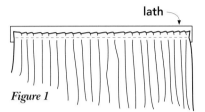

Figure 1

5 Gently gather the fabric onto the lath between the center and the ends, adjusting the gathers with your hands until they are even and straight.

6 Holding both ends of the lath in your hands with the right side of the fabric facing you, roll the lath away from you, until the lath is now upside-down and you can no longer see the staples, as shown in figure 2. Fit the lath against the edge on one side of the plywood top, then use the 1-inch (2.5 cm) finishing nails to nail through the fabric and the center of the lath into the plywood top.

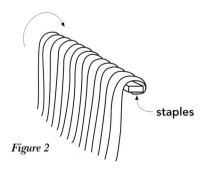

Figure 2

7 Adjust the gathers evenly, and nail through both ends of the lath. Add two more nails between the previous three to secure the lath to the top. Pull the fabric gently until the nails are no longer visible.

8 Repeat steps 1 through 7 to drape the remaining side of the dressing table.

Adding the Front Drape

1 Cut a piece of lath measuring the same length as the front of the fabric-covered top.

2 Attach two widths of 54-inch (1.37 m) fabric across the lath, using the same procedure that you used to make the side drapes.

3 Rather than nail the front drape to the plywood top, we used adhesive-backed hook-and-loop tape so that the front drape can be removed easily. Simply cut a length of hook-and-loop tape the same length as the lath and apply it over the edge of the plywood top. Next, remove the backing and attach the fabric-covered lath to the exposed adhesive side of the hook-and-loop tape.

4 Arrange the bottom of the side and front drapes to puddle evenly on the floor.

Making the Canopy

1 Cut a canopy top from 1 x 12 pine, measuring 36 inches (.9 m) long.

2 Cut a piece of quilt batting measuring 40 by 14 inches (101.5 x 35.5 cm). Place the quilt batting over the canopy top, wrap it over the edges, and staple it to the underside of the wood.

3 Cut a piece of fabric measuring 40 by 14 inches (101.5 x 35.5 cm). Center the fabric over the quilt batting, and staple it to the underside of the wood. Use enough staples to hold the fabric evenly and securely in place. You can minimize the number of wrinkles if you start by stapling the center of one long side, then the center of the opposite long side. Then work your way out toward the ends, smoothing the fabric as you go. Next, staple the center of each of the ends, and again work your way out to the corners. Ease the fabric over the corners, eliminating as many wrinkles as possible.

4 Measure the distance from your ceiling to the floor, and add 1 yard (.9 m). Cut two canopy side panels to that measurement. Because we used a sheer fabric that is 105 inches (2.6 m) wide, we cut only one canopy side panel and then cut it in half lengthwise to give us two equal panels.

5 Measure and mark one canopy side panel 22 inches (56 cm) from one end, as shown in figure 3.

Figure 3

22"
(56 cm)

6 Gather the side panel along your mark, and staple the gathers to the wrong side of the end of the canopy top, as shown in figure 4.

22" (56 cm)

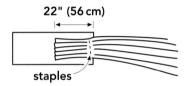

staples

Figure 4

7 Double the remaining 22 inches (56 cm) of fabric back over itself, and gather and staple the raw edges over your previous staples, to form a "poof" in the side panel.

8 Repeat steps 5 through 7 to gather and attach the remaining side panel to the opposite end of the canopy top.

9 To attach the canopy to the ceiling, decide where you want your dressing table, then center the canopy top over the dressing table. We simply nailed the canopy top to the ceiling using several 2½-inch-long (6.25 cm) finishing nails. Gently pull the fabric over the nails until they are no longer visible.

ROSE VANITY LAMP

A glass ginger-jar lamp, some potpourri, silk roses, and approximately one hour's time will give you this lovely decorative accent. You can cover the shade entirely with roses, or place a few here and there as you please.

INSTRUCTIONS

Filling the Lamp

1 Most purchased lamps come with instructions on how to disassemble them. If yours does not, use the pliers to simply remove the nut at the center bottom, and the lamp should come apart.

2 Fill the jar section of the lamp with the potpourri. Err on the side of overfilling the lamp; once you turn the lamp over, the potpourri will tend to settle over time.

3 Carefully replace the lamp bottom and secure the assembly in place by tightening the nut.

Covering the Lampshade

1 Carefully pull each of the silk roses from its stem. To keep the roses intact after they are removed, apply hot glue to the center bottom of each rose.

2 Beginning at the top of the lampshade, position and glue the roses around the lampshade, making certain that the petals entirely cover the top edge of the shade.

3 Add a second row of roses just below the first, again working around the shade.

4 Continue adding roses until you have completely covered the shade. You can cover the entire shade with just roses, or add some leaves, as we did.

MATERIALS

Purchased clear-glass ginger-jar lamp—ours measures 15 inches (37.5 cm) tall, including the lampshade

1 large bag of potpourri in colors to coordinate with your room

Enough silk roses in a coordinating color to cover your lampshade—we used one large bunch

TOOLS

Pliers

Scissors

Hot glue gun and glue sticks

FAMILY ROOM

Relax, renew yourself, and enjoy. The family room rivals the kitchen as the space that holds the best of family memories. When you are watching movies together, playing board games, or telling stories, you want a room that is comfortable, casual, and colorful. A cozy sofa throw, a soft pillow, and a fabric-lined cabinet to hold family finds and treasures, will help you create just the right environment. The fabric-covered wall gives the room extra warmth by combining color and texture.

FABRIC-COVERED WALL

If hanging wallpaper can't solve your wall's problems—cover it with fabric! Consider this hope for hopeless walls. Now you can cover holes, bumps and other unsightly areas. Aside from being a practical solution, it provides you with a luxurious textural option.

INSTRUCTIONS

Determining the Amount of Fabric

To make things easier, we suggest that you pick a medium-weight 54-inch-wide (1.37 m) fabric with no discernible pattern. If you choose a patterned fabric, you will have to contend with matching the fabric repeat which will take much more fabric.

First measure the length and height of the wall you will be covering. Since the fabric is 54 inches (1.37 m) wide (not counting the selvage), you can divide the total length of the wall by 54 (1.37) to determine the number of panels you will need for your project. Then measure from the floor to the ceiling to determine the length of each panel.

Multiply the number of panels needed by the length of each panel, and you have the amount of fabric you need. To allow enough fabric to cover the strips of lath, add the length of one more panel to the total measurement.

Determining the Amount of Lath

Since the sides, top, and bottom of each panel are hidden by fabric-covered lath strips, you will need to determine the total linear amount of lath needed for the project. You'll need the same number of vertical lath strips as the number of panels, plus one extra for the end. Then you'll need twice the length of the wall for the horizontal lath. When measuring, always remember to factor in a little more to your total for waste allowance.

Covering the Wall

1 Use a long level to divide and mark your wall, floor to ceiling, in 54-inch-wide (1.37 m) segments across its entire length.

2 Beginning on one side of your wall, staple a length of fabric across the top of the first marked segment. Check to make sure the fabric is hanging exactly straight. Use the marks you made in step 1 to guide the sides of the fabric as you work. When the top is straight, begin stapling the sides, working down from the top to the bottom of the wall, always keeping the fabric taut but not stretched out of shape. Trim the bottom of the panel close to the floor (or baseboard), and staple the fabric to the wall across the bottom of the panel.

3 Continue adding fabric panels across the length of the wall, overlapping the selvages where the panels meet.

MATERIALS

Medium-weight, 54-inch-wide (1.37 m) fabric of your choice—see *Determining the Amount of Fabric* below

Wood lath for covering the fabric seams—see *Determining the Amount of Lath* below

Finishing nails, 1½-inches (3.8 cm) long

TOOLS

Level

Scissors

Staple gun and staples

Utility knife

Glue gun and glue sticks

Hammer

4 Measure and cut the first vertical strip of lath. Lath can be cut easily with a utility knife.

5 Cut a strip of fabric 2 inches (5 cm) longer and 2 inches (5 cm) wider than the lath strip.

6 Lay the fabric strip right side down on a flat work surface, and center the lath on the fabric. Wrap the raw edges of the fabric strip over the edges of the lath, and glue them in place, using a glue gun.

7 Position the fabric-wrapped lath strip over the stapled vertical seam between the fabric wall panels. Use a level to make sure it is straight , then use the hammer and the 1½-inch (3.8 cm) nails to nail through the lath strip into the wall. Continue nailing the lath strip along the entire height of the wall, spacing the nails approximately 12 inches (30 cm) apart. To hide the nails when you are finished, pull the fabric gently around each nail until the nail head disappears.

8 Repeat steps 4 through 7 to cover and attach the remaining lath strips over all of the remaining vertical seams. Be sure to measure each one individually, since distances can vary.

9 Next, follow the same general procedures in steps 4 through 7 for measuring, covering, and nailing both the top and bottom horizontal lath strips to the top and bottom of the wall.

BOOK LAMP

Make this occasional lamp from real books, then use it in an office, family room, or library. (We've gotten many compliments on ours.) For variety, choose children's books to make a smaller version for the nursery.

INSTRUCTIONS

1 Select the books you want to use, then stack them, placing the largest book on the bottom, and the smallest one on the top. We turned some of our books at a slight angle to add some interest.

2 Mark the center of each book. To find the center, first use a ruler and pencil to draw a line that connects two opposite corners of the book. Repeat the process, drawing a line that connects the two remaining corners. The intersection of the two lines is the center of the book.

3 Drill a hole through the center of each book using a drill bit the same size as the lamp pipe. It is easier to drill through the book if you first clamp it to a work surface.

4 Restack the books in their proper order, then fit the lamp pipe through the center of the stack. Secure the pipe on the top and bottom with a nut. The bottom nut and pipe should be as flush as possible.

5 Follow the manufacturer's instructions in the lamp kit for wiring the lamp.

6 Place several protective plastic pads on the bottom of the lamp to lift it slightly above the tabletop.

7 Place the lampshade on the lamp.

MATERIALS

Assorted books*

Lamp kit—a pre-packaged kit containing everything needed for making a lamp**

Small, adhesive, protective pads for the bottom of the lamp—the round plastic ones work best

Lampshade—we suggest that you make the lamp, then take it with you when selecting the shade

TOOLS

Ruler

Pencil

Drill and drill bit the same diameter as the lamp pipe

Pliers

We used books that we already had, but you can find inexpensive books at garage sales. Give some thought to the color of books you select. You don't want a lamp made of bright orange books if you intend to use it in a predominantly pink room.

**Make certain that the kit includes a lamp pipe (the pipe that will go through the middle of the books) that is long enough to accommodate the height of your finished lamp. If the pipe isn't long enough, you will have to purchase another one separately.*

SOFA THROW

If you have as many pets and people on your sofa as we do, you'll appreciate this easy-to-make throw—it has saved our family-room sofa from many potential catastrophes. Even if you make it from dry-clean-only fabric, it is certainly less expensive to clean a throw than an entire sofa.

MATERIALS

2 yards (1.8 m) of 54-inch-wide (1.37 m) fabric in a color of your choice

Iron-on seam tape

TOOLS

Ruler or tape measure

Scissors

Iron and ironing board

INSTRUCTIONS

1 Cut a 2-yard (1.8 m) length of a 54-inch-wide (1.37 cm) fabric of your choice. We used the same plaid fabric that we used for our family room curtains.

2 Use iron-on seam tape to make a 1-inch (2.5 cm) hem on each of the two raw edges.

3 Use iron-on seam tape to make a 1-inch (2.5 cm) hem on each of the two selvage edges. Throw it on your sofa and enjoy!

FRINGED PILLOW

Even if you don't know how to sew, you can make this pillow in no time—it's all put together with iron-on seam tape and hot glue. Add some bullion fringe, and it will look like it came from a decorator's shop.

MATERIALS

1 yard (.9 m) of 54-inch-wide (1.37 m) fabric—we used a plaid to match our other family room accessories.

2½ yards (2.3 m) of bullion fringe in a coordinating color

1 pillow form, 18 inches (45 cm) square

1 roll of iron-on seam tape

TOOLS

Tape measure

Scissors

Iron and ironing board

Glue gun and glue sticks

INSTRUCTIONS

1 Cut two fabric squares, each measuring 24 inches (61 cm).

2 Use iron-on seam tape to make a 1-inch (2.5 cm) hem on all four edges of each of the fabric squares.

3 Place the two hemmed fabric squares wrong sides together. Cut a length of iron-on seam tape that is the length of three sides of the fabric square, and place it between the two squares, slightly in from the edges. Iron the squares together on three sides, leaving one side open.

4 Slip the pillow form inside. Use a length of iron-on seam tape to close the remaining opening.

5 Beginning at the center of one side, use the hot glue to glue bullion fringe around the outside of the pillow.

FABRIC-LINED CABINET

If you have an old cupboard or cabinet that could use some sprucing up, cover the inside with fabric to coordinate with your color scheme. It's simple to do, and provides the perfect backdrop for your favorite collectibles.

INSTRUCTIONS

Making the Patterns

1 Remove the cabinet shelves, if possible. If it is not possible, you will need to treat each opening as five different surfaces (top, bottom, two sides, and back), and will need to cut a separate pattern for each of them. Since each of the patterns will be covered with fabric, you need to cut a separate pattern for each surface, even if two surfaces are the identical size.

2 Carefully measure each of the surfaces of the cabinet. Using a metal straight edge and a craft or utility knife, cut a separate piece of poster board for each surface. Check for fit after cutting each piece by placing it in the cabinet. Mark each piece so that you can tell where the pattern fits in the cabinet, and which edge is "up." When marking the patterns for the horizontal surfaces (top and bottom), mark "up" on the edge where they meet the back surface.

3 If you are using a heavyweight fabric, cut the poster board patterns slightly smaller than the actual dimensions of the cabinet surfaces; this will allow for the additional space taken when the fabric is wrapped around the pattern pieces.

Figuring the Material

1 Place the patterns on a large flat work surface with each of the "up" marks facing in the same direction. Allow for a 1-inch (2.5 cm) allowance on all four sides of each pattern. Arrange the patterns so that they will fit within a 54-inch (1.37 m) width to simulate the width of the fabric you will be using.

2 Measure the length of the total pattern layout, and you will have the total amount of fabric you need to line your cabinet. Since you will also be covering the wood-trim strips, factor in a little additional fabric for this.

Covering the Patterns

1 Place the length of fabric on a large work surface. Place each of the patterns on top of the fabric in the same positions that you used when you measured for the fabric. Again, make sure that your "up" arrows all face in the same direction, and that you have a 1-inch (2.5 cm) allowance around all four sides of each pattern piece. Use masking tape to keep the patterns in position. Cut out each of the pattern pieces, making sure you cut 1 inch (2.5 cm) from the edge of the pattern piece.

2 Fold the 1-inch (2.5 cm) fabric border around the edges of each of the pattern pieces and press carefully with an iron. Since you want the pattern piece to lie as flat as possible, trim out the corners of the fabric to avoid any lumpy layers.

3 Check the front of the panel to make certain that there are no wrinkles in the fabric. Use a hot glue gun to secure the pressed border to the back side of the pattern.

4 Continue the process until you have covered all of the patterns, and have a finished fabric panel for each of your cabinet surfaces.

Installing the Panels

1 Always install the "back" fabric panel first, securing it to the cabinet with hot glue or spray adhesive.

2 Install the side fabric panels next, also securing them with glue or adhesive. Install the top and bottom panels.

Trimming the Front Edges

1 Measure and cut strips of 1-inch (2.5 cm) screen molding to fit around the outer edges of the fabric-

MATERIALS

Heavy poster board—enough to make patterns for each of the surfaces you will be covering

54-inch-wide (1.37 m) fabric—enough for each of the patterns you make*

1-inch (2.5 cm) screen molding—enough to cover the edges of your finished cabinet

TOOLS

Tape measure

Pencil

Straightedge

Craft or utility knife

Masking tape

Iron

Hot glue gun and glue sticks

Spray adhesive (optional)

Finishing nails (optional)

*Since most cabinets are not perfectly square, we suggest that you avoid selecting a geometric pattern.

lined cabinet. Screen molding is very thin, and can be cut with an ordinary utility knife.

2 Cut a piece of fabric 2 inches (5 cm) wider and 2 inches (5 cm) longer than each of your screen molding strips.

3 Wrap each of the strips in fabric, securing the fabric on the back, using hot glue.

4 Attach each of the strips to your cabinet to hide the edges of your fabric panels. Use hot glue or small finishing nails to hold them in place. If you use nails, pull gently on the fabric until the nail head is no longer visible.

FABRIC-COVERED LAMP

Here's a quick-fix for that incredibly ugly lamp from your favorite aunt—just wrap it with fabric, add some satin cord, and presto, a brand new coordinated lamp!

INSTRUCTIONS

1 Place the fabric right side down on your work surface. Center the lamp base on top of the fabric, then trace around the base with a pencil.

2 Draw a straight line on the fabric from the point where the lamp cord emerges from the side of the lamp to the edge of the fabric, as shown in figure 1.

3 Remove the lamp from the fabric, and cut the fabric only along the straight line that you drew in step 2.

4 Fold the fabric wrong sides together on both sides of the cut, as shown in figure 2, then press in place. Secure the fabric with hot glue.

5 This next step will be easier if you can enlist the assistance of a helper. Replace the lamp on the traced base, making sure that the lamp cord is matched to the hemmed slit in the fabric. Gather all sides of the fabric around the top of the lamp, then very tightly tie the gathers with string or lightweight wire. Adjust the gathers until they are even around the entire lamp.

6 Leave a "ruffle" of fabric that extends approximately 2 inches (5 cm) from the top of the base. Cut off any excess fabric.

7 Tie a satin cord around the top of the lamp to cover the string or wire, then tie the ends in a bow.

MATERIALS

1½ yards (1.37 m) of 54-inch-wide (1.37 m) fabric—we chose a plaid to coordinate with our room*

1 old lamp (the uglier, the better!), no larger than 50 inches (1.27 m) measured down from the top of the lamp base, across the bottom, and back up to the top of the opposite side of the base

String or lightweight wire

1 yard (.9 m) of satin cord in a color that coordinates with your fabric

TOOLS

Flat work surface

Pencil

Scissors

Glue gun and glue sticks

Ruler or measuring tape

You will need to select a fairly stiff fabric for this project to form the "ruffle" at the top of the lamp.

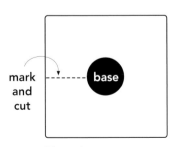

Figure 1

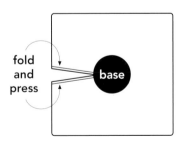

Figure 2

UPHOLSTERED CHAIRS

To coordinate our family room, we recovered two old chairs. We were pleased with the results, and surprised at the short amount of time it took us to complete the project. Just a note of reassurance: reupholstering is really very easy to do if you think it through and take your time.

MATERIALS

Old chair

Enough 54-inch-wide (1.37 m) fabric to cover your particular chair

Upholstery braid—enough ½-inch (1.3 cm) braid to cover the raw edges of the fabric*

1 bag of quilt batting (if needed) for filling dips and depressions

TOOLS

Tape measure

Scissors

Straight pins

Staple gun and staples

Glue gun and glue sticks

*If you can easily remove the braid from the old chair, do so, then measure it to find out how much new braid to purchase. Otherwise, measure the area where you want to place the braid to determine how much you will need.

INSTRUCTIONS

Surveying the Project

To upholster a piece of furniture, you must logically think through the project before you begin. The previous upholstery job will provide a starting place. Inspect the corners or other tricky areas to determine how they were folded or pleated. Also take note of any "dips" or "swaybacks" in the chair, and fill these depressions as needed, as you work with quilt batting. Don't be intimidated by the process. If you work slowly and thoughtfully, you'll be proud of your finished job.

Upholstering the Chair

1 Measure the seat and back of the chair. To each measurement, add a 3-inch (7.5 cm) allowance on all sides. Cut the fabric to these measurements.

2 If necessary, add quilt batting to the seat to fill in any depressions.

3 Center the fabric over the seat, and temporarily hold it in place, using straight pins.

4 Begin stapling the fabric to the chair frame, using enough staples to hold the fabric evenly and securely in place. As you work, use the scissors to trim the fabric just outside the staples. Since you will be covering the staples with the upholstery braid, try to keep the staples in a fairly uniform line. You can minimize the number of wrinkles if you start by stapling the center of one side, then the center of the opposite side. Then work your way out toward the corners, smoothing the fabric as you go. Next, staple the center of each of the remaining sides, and again work your way out toward the corners. Ease the fabric over the corners, eliminating as many wrinkles as possible. Finish the corners in the same manner as the old upholstery. If your stapler is too large for some areas of the chair, use a glue gun and hot glue to secure the fabric.

5 Finish the job by gluing upholstery braid over the staples and the raw edges of your fabric.

FIREPLACE SCREEN

What do you do with your fireplace in the summertime? If you are faced with hiding an unattractive or unused fireplace, make a fabric-covered screen. While it's not very practical or safe to use during the winter, you'll find the screen is a welcome addition to your room during the off-season when you cover it in a fabric that coordinates with your room.

INSTRUCTIONS

1 Cut four pieces from the pine board, each measuring 25 inches (63.5 cm) long. These will be your panels.

2 Cut eight pieces from your chosen fabric, each measuring 29 by 12 inches (73.5 x 30 cm).

3 Place one piece of fabric right side down on a flat work surface. Center one wood panel over the fabric rectangle. Fold all four edges of the fabric rectangle over the edges of the wood panel and use a glue gun to hold them in place. You can minimize the number of wrinkles if you start by gluing the center of one long side, then the center of the opposite long side. Then work your way out toward the ends, smoothing the fabric as you go. Next, glue the center of each of the ends, and again work your way out toward the corners. Neatly fold the fabric over the corners, eliminating as many wrinkles as possible.

4 Cut off any excess fabric—you want the back of the panel to be as flat as possible.

5 Fold, then press in hems on all four sides of a second fabric panel until the hemmed size of the panel measures 24¾ by 7 inches (63 x 17.5 cm). Note that these hems are made specifically generous. Use iron-on seam tape to secure the hems.

6 Place the hemmed piece of fabric over the uncovered back of the wood panel. Use hot glue to attach it over the raw edges of the fabric applied in step 3.

7 Repeat steps 3 through 6 three more times, using the remaining wood panels and fabric pieces.

Finishing

1 Place the four completed screens right side down on a flat work surface. Make sure they are parallel to each other and that the 25-inch-long (63.5 cm) sides meet.

2 Install the hinges. Use two hinges for each joint between the screens, positioning them 3 inches (7.5 cm) from the top and bottom.

NOTE: You have two options if you need to make a wider screen. You could substitute 1 x 12 pine for the 1 x 8 pine. Or, you could simply make and add more panels.

MATERIALS

9 linear feet (2.75 m) of 1 x 8 pine cut in four pieces, each measuring 25 inches (63.5 cm) long*

3 yards (2.75 m) of 54-inch-wide (1.37 m) fabric in the color of your choice

6 brass hinges, each 1-inch (2.5 cm) long

TOOLS

Saw (if you plan to cut the wood yourself)

Measuring tape

Scissors

Flat work surface

Glue gun and glue sticks

Iron and ironing board

Iron-on seam tape

Screwdriver

If you don't have the tools to cut the boards yourself, most lumberyards and home centers will cut them for you at a nominal cost.

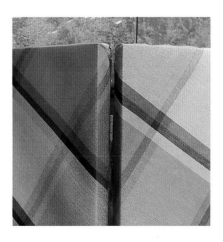

PLEATED WINDOW TREATMENT

Here's a way to add treatments along a wall of windows without obstruct-ing the view. We added a pleated valance above the windows, then covered ordinary 2 x 4 pine with fabric to add interest between the windows. To finish it off, we installed gathered drapes at either side. Because our drapes cover a very sunny window, we added sheers to cut the glare.

MATERIALS

54-inch-wide (1.37 cm) fabric—see *Determining the Amount of Fabric* below to find out how much you will need

Bullion fringe—see *Deter-mining the Amount of Fab-ric* below to find out how much you will need

2 x 4 pine, enough for between each window and to span the width of the valance—see *Measuring for Lumber* below

Several 3 by 3½-inch (7.5 x 8.8 cm) blocks, cut from scrap pine—see *Mea-suring for Lumber* below

1¼-inch (3 cm) nails, approximately 20 to 30

2½-inch (6.5 cm) nails, approximately 15 to 20

Iron-on seam tape

TOOLS

Tape Measure
Large flat work surface
Scissors
Hammer
Straight pins
Staple gun and staples
Glue gun and glue sticks
Level

INSTRUCTIONS

Determining the Amount of Fabric

VALANCE

First, measure the total width of the valance you will be making (this is the span of your window plus any exten-sions beyond both sides). Then decide the finished depth of your valance, which will be the length of the pleats. Since you need to attach the valance to a support board, you will need to add 2 inches (5 cm) to the measurement for the desired finished length. For example, if you want the finished valance (pleats) to be 12 inches (30 cm) long, add 2 inches (5 cm) to that measurement to get 14 inches (35 cm).

Next, decide the width you desire for each of the finished pleats. (As shown in the photograph, our fin-ished pleats are each 5½ inches [13.8 cm] wide.) Make a paper pat-tern to the chosen length and width of the pleats by actually folding the pleats in the paper—you only need to fold several pleats. When the pattern is folded to your specifications, mark a 2-foot (24-inch [61 cm]) length on

the folded pattern. Then unfold the pattern and measure between the marks. Divide that measurement in half to give you the actual yardage you need for each foot (12-inches [30 cm]) of the total width of your valance. Add approximately 8 inches (20 cm) to the total measurement, to allow for hemming and turning the corners at each end of the valance.

You will cut the fabric for the valance on the straight of the fabric (the grain), giving you a relatively long narrow piece of fabric. You will use the remainder of the fabric to cover the boards that will be placed between the windows.

To help you determine the fabric you will need, use the valance as shown as a reference. Because the total width of our window treatment is almost 9 feet (2.75 m), our valance required 11 running yards (10 m) of plaid fabric. Since we wanted a fin-ished length of 12 inches (30.3 cm), we cut a long strip 14 inches (35 cm) wide. We took advantage of the size of the plaid's repeat to determine the 5½-inch (13.8 cm) finished width of our pleats.

THE SIDE DRAPES

To determine the necessary material for the side drapes, measure the length from the floor to a point that will be at least 6 inches (15 cm) above the bottom of the finished valance. Multiply that measurement by two, and you have the yardage for both drapes.

BULLION FRINGE

The fringe will trim the bottom of the valance and the bottom of the side drapes. For the valance, you will need the same number of yards of fringe as you need for the total width of your valance. For the side drapes, you will need 108 inches (2.7 m) of fringe for each of the two 54-inch-wide (1.37 m) panels.

MEASURING FOR LUMBER

Two-by-four pine comes in various lengths. You need to purchase enough boards to span the width of the valance. Two boards can be joined if necessary. For the pieces between the windows, measure the length from the baseboard to a point which will be at least 6 inches (15 cm) above the bottom of the valance. Purchase the number of boards you need in a long enough length. When you are purchasing the wood for this project, it is very important that it is not warped or bowed. Search until you find boards that are straight along the entire length. To check for warping or bowing before you buy, place one end of the board on the floor and look down its length. Then turn the board and look down the edge. Your own eye is the best test.

To attach the valance to the wall, you'll need several blocks approximately 3 by 3½ inches (7.5 x 8.8 cm) in size. You will need approximately one block for every 24 inches (61 cm) of valance. These can be cut from the waste of the 2 x 4s. If you can't cut them yourself, most home centers will cut them for you for a nominal charge.

Making the Valance

1 Cut a board the length of your valance. If it is necessary to piece two boards together, use the 1½-inch (3.8 cm) nails to nail a wood block over the joint, using at least two nails on each side of the joint, as shown in figure 1. Using the 1½-inch (3.8 cm) nails, nail additional wood blocks to each end of the valance support board(s), then nail additional blocks along its length, spacing them approximately every 24 inches (61 cm).

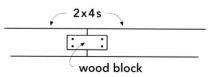

Figure 1

2 Cut a valance from the fabric of your choice. As shown, our valance was 11 yards long (10 m) and 14 inches (35 cm) wide.

3 Use iron-on seam tape to make a 1-inch (2.5 cm) hem on both short ends of the valance.

4 Begin pleating the valance across the length of your board(s). You may want to pleat the raw, cut edge of the fabric to the board and allow the selvage edge, which is more finished, to be the bottom edge of the valance. We suggest that you use straight pins to hold the pleats in place temporarily, until you have pleated the entire valance; you can then adjust the individual pleat width or the pleat placement across the support if necessary.

5 When you are satisfied that your pleat placement is even and straight across the valance, attach the fabric valance to the support, using a staple gun and staples. Staple each side of every pleat to the top edge and back of the support board.

6 Use a glue gun to attach the bullion fringe to the bottom edge of the valance.

Making the Side Drapes

1 Cut a length of fabric that is measured from the floor to a point which will be at least 6 inches (15 cm) above the bottom of the valance. Use a glue gun to attach bullion fringe to the bottom of the drape. Repeat to make a second drape.

2 Gather the top raw edge of the drape with your hands, and position it to the outside of the outer window. Use a staple gun to attach the drape directly to the wall, as shown in figure 2. Repeat the procedure to attach the remaining drape to the opposite outer window. Note: We chose to position our drape on the outside of the window frame. You may prefer to position the drapes to the inside.

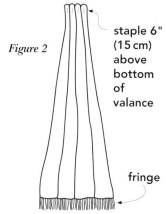

Figure 2

staple 6"
(15 cm)
above
bottom
of
valance

fringe

Making the Trim Between Windows

1 Cut a board to the length from the baseboard to a point which will be at least 6 inches (15 cm) above the bottom of the valance.

2 Cut a piece of fabric that is 6 inches (15 cm) wider and 8 inches (20 cm) longer than your board.

3 Place the fabric right side down on a flat work surface. Place the board in the center of the fabric.

4 Staple the fabric to the board, working from the center out toward both ends. If you are using a plaid or a geometric print, pay particular attention to the placement of the fabric on the board, making sure all vertical and horizontal lines are straight. Repeat steps 1 through 4 to make the necessary number of trims needed between your windows.

5 To attach the trim pieces, we simply nailed through the trims into the wall, using 2½-inch-long (6.25 cm) nails. Before nailing, use a level to make sure that your placement of the trim is exactly vertical. To hide the nails, pull gently on the fabric around each nail until the nail head disappears.

Hanging the Valance

You will probably require some assistance with this step if your valance is very wide. We suggest you use a level to make certain that your valance is straight across the windows. When the valance is level, lift the fabric out of the way, and, using the 2½-inch (6.25 cm) nails, nail through the valance support and through each of the wood blocks into the wall.

SPONGE-PAINTED CHAIRS

When our off-white upholstered chairs started looking grimy, we came up with an ingenious solution—we would just sponge paint over them, making sure we covered the dirty parts with paint. We figured if our idea didn't work, we would be no worse off, and would just have them reupholstered. Well, we're pretty proud of the result, and hope that you might be able to use the idea somewhere in your house.

MATERIALS

Dirty chairs*

Latex paint in colors of your choice**

TOOLS

Drop cloth or other protection for your work surface

Rubber gloves

Paper or plastic plate

Sea sponge

Newspapers

Our chairs were covered in an off-white duck fabric. We imagine almost any fabric would be a candidate for this technique. We're not certain the results would be as good if you sponge-painted over a heavily textured fabric. However, if your chairs look as bad as ours did, there is little to lose if it doesn't work out.

**Judging from our experiment, it is better to stay as close as possible to the original shade of color on the chairs, even if you pick another color. We chose a very pale green for our off-white chairs. If we had chosen a darker color, we think the contrast would have been too great.*

INSTRUCTIONS

1 Place the chair in the center of a drop cloth, and don your rubber gloves.

2 Pour a small amount of paint on a paper or plastic plate.

3 Wet the sponge thoroughly with water, and dip one side of it into the paint on the plate.

4 Blot the sponge on a newspaper. The idea is to remove the excess paint from the sponge so that the sponge pattern doesn't look like a giant blob of paint, allowing you to see the texture.

5 Press the sponge onto the chair fabric, turning your hand as you work so that the sponge produces different patterns. If you hold your sponge still, you'll just repeat the same pattern every time.

6 Sponge the entire chair, and let it dry overnight.

FABRIC-COVERED TABLE

Since we needed a larger table for our family room, we covered a small, rather dilapidated soda-fountain table with fabric, then placed a larger piece of glass on the top. Now it coordinates with the room—and we can seat four people comfortably around it.

DINING ROOM

We wanted our dining room to reflect our relaxed lifestyle. With a few simple touches, we've created a space that puts any guest instantly at ease. The treatment for the French doors is both easy to make and colorful. With little effort, we quickly coordinated the chairs and placemats—just in time for dinner.

FRENCH-DOOR TREATMENT

French doors always present a special window-treatment challenge—you want to frame the window, but still be able to open and close the doors. We solved the problem handsomely with a valance of varied-colored triangles.

INSTRUCTIONS

Making the Valance

1 Cut two lengths of fabric, one red and one purple, each measuring 10½ feet (3.2 m) long and 12 inches (30 cm) wide.

2 Place the purple fabric, right side down, on a flat work surface. Center one 10-foot-long (3 m) piece of 2 x 4 pine over the purple fabric. Wrap the raw edges of the fabric strip over the edges of the wood, overlapping them where they meet, then staple them in place. Fold both the ends neatly to the stapled side of the board, and staple the ends in place.

3 Repeat step 2 to cover the remaining 10-foot-long (3 m) piece of 2 x 4 pine, using the red fabric.

4 Fold the 26-inch (66 cm) burgundy square in half, then bring the top two folded corners to the center of the unfolded edge to form a triangle, as shown in figure 1.

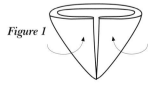

Figure 1

5 Repeat step 4, using the remaining two purple squares and the smaller four green squares.

6 Center the folded burgundy triangle (folded edges down) over the stapled side of the purple fabric-covered 2 x 4. The raw edges of the triangle should face the center of the 2 x 4, as shown in figure 2. Staple the triangle in place.

Figure 2

7 Add the remaining six triangles, following the order shown in the photograph: two greens outside the burgundy, then two purples, and two more greens. When you are pleased with the placement, staple each of the triangles to the fabric-covered 2 x 4.

8 Nail the red fabric-covered 2 x 4, staple side down, over the purple fabric-covered 2 x 4. Nail through the top 2 x 4 into the bottom one, using six 2½-inch-long (6.25 cm) finishing nails.

MATERIALS*

Two 10-foot (3 m) lengths of 2 x 4 pine

Two lengths of fabric measuring 10½ feet (3.2 m) long and 12 inches (30 cm) wide, one in purple and one in red fabric**

7 fabric squares—one burgundy and two purple, each 26 inches (66 cm) square; and four green each 14 inches (35 cm) square

Two 3½-inch (8.8 cm) lengths of 2 x 4 pine

Two 3½-inch (8.8 cm) lengths of 1 x 4 pine

10 finishing nails, 2½-inches (6.25 cm) long

Two lengths of 54-inch-wide (1.37 m) purple fabric, each 9 feet (2.75 m) long

5 L-brackets

Molly bolts (if necessary)

1⅝-inch (4 cm) screws

½-inch (1.9 cm) screws

TOOLS

Measuring tape

Flat work surface

Staple gun and staples

Level

The materials specified are enough to construct a 10-foot-wide (3 m) valance with two side drapes that accommodate an 8-foot-high (2.4 m) ceiling. The size of the valance can be adjusted by adding or subtracting the number of triangles, or by changing the size of the individual triangles.

**If you have access to a sewing machine, you can piece several lengths of fabric together.*

Adding the Side Finials

1 Cover the two 2 x 4 blocks with burgundy fabric, using the same technique that you used to cover the 10-foot-long (3 m) 2 x 4s.

2 Cover the 1 x 4 blocks with green fabric, using the same technique.

3 Nail a burgundy block over one end of the assembled valance, with the stapled side facing the valance. Use two 2½-inch (6.25 cm) finishing nails to secure it in place.

4 Place one green fabric block (stapled side in) over one burgundy block. Nail through the green block, using two 2½-inch (6.25 cm) finishing nails.

Adding the Side Drapes

1 For the drape, cut two lengths of fabric, each the same measurement as your floor-to- ceiling measurement.

2 Gather the top raw edge of one drape with your hands, and position it to the outside of the outer door where the top of the drape will be covered by the valance. Use a staple gun to attach the drape directly to the wall, as shown in Figure 3. Repeat the procedure for the other drape on the opposite wall.

Hanging the Valance

1 To hang the valance, attach the L-brackets to the wall over the French door. If necessary, use molly bolts to hold them in place. Make sure that the top of the valance will fit between the L-brackets and the ceiling, and that the brackets are exactly level. Use 1⅝-inch (4 cm) screws to attach the brackets into the wall.

2 Find someone to help you place the valance top over the L-brackets. Under the valance, use ½-inch (1.3 cm) screws to attach the valance to the L-brackets.

MATERIALS

Fabric cut in rectangles that are the size of the finished place mats, plus a 1-inch (2.5 cm) allowance on all four sides—we wanted a larger-than-ordinary placemat, so we cut each rectangle 16 x 22 inches (40 x 56 cm)*

Iron-on seam tape

Length of fringe twice the length of the finished sides of the placemat (optional).

TOOLS

Measuring tape

T-square or framing square

Scissors

Iron and ironing board

Hot glue and glue sticks (optional)

We suggest you use a fairly lightweight fabric for this project, since the hems need to be turned twice—a heavy fabric would make the edges of the placemat too bulky.

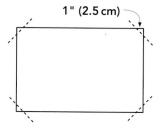

Figure 1

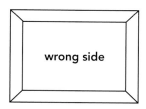

PLACEMATS

Here's an easy and inexpensive way to dress up your table—make your own coordinated placemats with leftover fabric from a window treatment or other project in the room. You'll find that when you make your own, you can size the placemats more generously than those you purchase in the store.

INSTRUCTIONS

1 Figure the finished size of the placemat. To that measurement, add a 1-inch (2.5 cm) allowance on all four sides. Use a T-square or framing square to make certain that all four corners are 90-degree angles. Cut a fabric rectangle for each placemat you will make.

2 Clip all four corners, as shown in Figure 1. Use iron-on seam tape to make a ½-inch (1.3 cm) hem in all four sides of the rectangle.

3 Again, use iron-on seam tape to make another ½-inch (1.3 cm) hem in all four sides of the rectangle, so that the raw edges of the previous hem made in step 2 are no longer visible. Fold the clipped corners as shown in figure 1.

4 If desired, use hot glue to glue a fringe down both sides of the finished place mat.

MATERIALS

Dining chair

Fabric the size of your chair seat, plus a 4-inch (10 cm) allowance on all sides

TOOLS

Measuring tape

Scissors

Flat work surface

Staple gun and staples

UPHOLSTERED CHAIRS

If you have dining room chairs, chances are the seat covers can be easily changed to go with any new color scheme. Most dining chairs can be unscrewed from the chair frame, covered with your fabric, then replaced.

INSTRUCTIONS

1 Remove the chair seat from the chair. There are usually four screws underneath each seat. Once you remove the screws, the chair seat should lift off easily.

2 Measure the length and width of the seat, add a 4-inch (10 cm) allowance to each side, then cut a piece of fabric to those dimensions.

3 Place the fabric right side down on a flat work surface. Center the seat upside down over the fabric.

4 Pull the fabric over the edges of the chair seat and staple it to the underside. Use enough staples to hold the fabric evenly and securely in place. You can minimize the number of wrinkles if you start by stapling the center of one long side, then the center of the opposite long side. Then work your way out toward the corners, smoothing the fabric as you go. Next, staple the center of each of the remaining sides, and again work your way out toward the corners. Ease the fabric over the corners, eliminating as many wrinkles as possible.

5 Replace the seat on the frame, screwing the seat to chair.

UPHOLSTERED STOOLS

You can easily recover stool seats to match your new color scheme. Just follow the general directions for covering your dining chairs.

GUEST ROOM

We love having guests stay over. We also love to provide them with a room that is both comfortable and cozy. The bed canopy warms the room while instantly filling it with flowers. The coordinating balloon curtains, ruffle-skirted side table, and comforter trim carries color throughout the room. And, what better way to pamper guests in the morning than with a fabric-lined tray bearing croissants and coffee.

BED CANOPY

Turn your bedroom into a romantic retreat with the addition of this beautiful canopy. Although it looks impressive and difficult to make, it actually requires very little skill to complete and can adorn your bed in no time.

INSTRUCTIONS

Determining the Amount of Fabric

Figure each measurement in steps 1 through 4 below, then add them together to determine the total amount of fabric you will need. The following will give you enough fabric to make a canopy for a queen-size bed; you will need to adjust your measurements for a smaller or larger bed.

1 To cover the canopy, you will need a piece of fabric that measures 86 x 21 inches (215 x 53.5 cm). If you are using a fabric with a pattern repeat that runs widthwise rather than lengthwise, you will need to use two widths across the canopy front, and allow for extra fabric to match the pattern.

2 For the side drapes, measure the distance from the ceiling to the floor, then add 12 inches (30 cm) to this measurement. Since you will be making two drapes, multiply that total by two.

3 To make the wall drape, measure the height of the wall starting 6 inches (15 cm) below the ceiling to the floor. Multiply that figure by three, since three panels are necessary for the drape. **NOTE:** If you want to save some fabric, cut the wall drapes shorter since the bottom will be hidden by the head of the bed.

4 You will need 1 yard (.9 m) of 54-inch-wide (1.37 cm) coordinating fabric for the front canopy ruffle (we used a deep lavender color).

Making the Canopy

1 Lay the 6-foot (1.8 m) length of 1 x 12 pine—the front of the canopy—on a large work surface. Make sure it lies flat.

2 Stand the 6-foot (1.8 m) piece of 1 x 6 pine—the top—on edge against one edge of the front, as shown in figure 1. Using the screwdriver and 1¼-inch (3 cm) screws, screw through the side of the top into the edge of the front, spacing the screws approximately 8 inches (20 cm) apart.

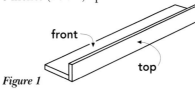

Figure 1

3 Fit the 1-foot (30 cm) pieces of 1 x 6 pine—the sides—over the exposed ends of the top and front, as shown in figure 2. Using the 1¼-inch (3 cm) screws, screw through the sides into the edges of the top and front.

Figure 2

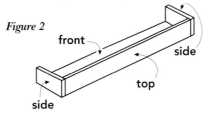

MATERIALS

6 linear feet (1.8 m) of 1 x 12 pine for the canopy front

8 linear feet (2.4 m) of 1 x 6 pine cut into three pieces: one 6 feet long (1.8 m) for the top, and two each 1 foot long (30 cm) for the sides*

1¼-inch (3 cm) screws, approximately 20

Two coordinating fabrics—see *Determining the Amount of Fabric* below

1 bag of quilt batting

Iron-on seam tape

5 sturdy 3-inch (7.5 cm) L-brackets with legs

Molly bolts

¾-inch (1.9 cm) screws

2 curtain tiebacks with attached tassels

2 curtain or cup hooks

TOOLS

Tape measure

Saw (if you are cutting the wood yourself)

Large flat work surface

Screwdriver

Scissors

Staple gun and staples

Glue gun and glue sticks

* If you don't have the tools to cut it yourself, most home centers and lumberyards will do so for a nominal charge.

4 Cut a piece of fabric 86 x 21 inches (215 x 53.5 cm). If you are using a fabric with a large pattern repeat, you will need to match the pattern, and seam two widths together.

5 Cut a piece of quilt batting 86 x 21 inches (215 x 53.5 cm).

6 Place the fabric right side down on a flat work surface, then place the quilt batting over it, aligning the edges. Center the wooden canopy frame over the batting with the bottom of the frame 2 inches (5 cm) from one 86-inch-long (215 cm) edge.

7 Wrap the 2 inches (5 cm) of fabric and batting to the inside of the canopy frame and staple them in place, working from the center out toward each of the ends. Use ample staples to keep the fabric and batting from puckering along the length.

8 Pull the opposite side of the fabric and batting over the front and top and staple it to the inside of the canopy. Again work from the center out toward the ends. When you reach the ends, staple the sides first, then pleat the fabric at the top of the canopy, and staple the ends inside the canopy.

Adding the Canopy Drapes and Ruffle Trim

NOTE: You may decide you do not want a ruffle on the front of your canopy as shown. If not, skip steps 1 through 5, and proceed to step 6 for making the side drapes.

1 We added a 4-inch (10 cm) ruffle to the bottom front of our canopy. To make the ruffle, cut three widths of 54-inch-wide (1.37 m) coordinated fabric, each measuring 10 inches (25 cm) long.

2 Using the iron-on seam tape, make a 1-inch (2.5 cm) hem along the two side (selvage) edges of each of the ruffles, as shown in figure 3.

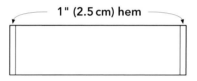
1" (2.5 cm) hem

Figure 3

3 Fold the hemmed ruffle lengthwise, with wrong sides together.

4 Lay the folded panel on a flat work surface. Gently gather the two top raw edges of the panel with your hands, until the panel width measures approximately 24 inches (61 cm) across the top. Keeping the raw edges straight and even, secure the gathers using hot glue.

5 Turn the canopy upside down. Beginning at one side, staple the first fabric ruffle inside the canopy front. The ruffle should overhang the canopy bottom by 4 inches (10 cm). Continue adding the remaining two

ruffles, slightly overlapping the previous ruffle each time.

6 To make a side drape, measure the distance from the ceiling to the floor and to that measurement, add 12 inches (30 cm). Cut the 54-inch-wide (1.37 m) fabric to that length.

7 Gather the width of the drape in your hands until it is approximately 4 inches (10 cm) wide, then staple the gathers to the inside of the canopy frame. Repeat steps 6 and 7 to attach a second drape to the remaining side of the canopy.

Adding the Wall Drape

1 Decide where you will position the canopy on your wall and mark a 6-foot-wide (1.8 m) space where it will hang.

2 Measure the height of the wall starting 6 inches (15 cm) below the ceiling to the floor. Cut three drape panels to that length from the 54-inch-wide (1.37 m) fabric.

3 Use iron-on tape to make a ½-inch (1.3 cm) hem along each of the side (selvage) edges of each panel.

4 Working on a flat surface, gather the raw edge of the drape top until it measures approximately 24 inches (61 cm) wide. Secure the gathers in place, using hot glue.

5 Staple the three gathered panels to the wall within the 6-foot (1.8 m) span marked in step 1. Attach the center panel first, and overlap the panels where they meet at the sides.

PILLOW COVERS

Make a pillow cover for any size bed pillow. If you can sew a straight seam, you can complete this project.

INSTRUCTIONS

Determining the Amount of Fabric

You will need one fabric rectangle for each pillow. To determine the amount of fabric you'll need, first measure the length and width of your pillow. To find the length of your fabric, multiply the length measurement of your pillow by 2½. Next find the width of your fabric by adding 2 inches (5 cm) to the width measurement of your pillow.

Finishing

1 To hang the canopy, first attach the L-brackets to the wall close to the ceiling, using molly bolts if necessary. Make sure that the top of the canopy will fit between the L-brackets and the ceiling, and that the five L-brackets are exactly level.

2 Find someone to help you, and slide the canopy top between the L-brackets and the ceiling. Inside the canopy, use ½-inch-long (1.9 cm) screws to attach the canopy to the brackets.

3 Gather a side drape with a curtain tieback and arrange it at the height you want. Attach a cup hook to the wall to hold the tieback. Repeat for the opposite side.

NOTE: You may want to add crown moulding around the top of your canopy. Our room already had crown moulding, so we added some to match. However, the canopy will look fine without it.

Making the Cover

1 Cut a fabric rectangle to the dimensions needed for your pillow.

2 Use iron-on seam tape to make a 1-inch (2.5 cm) hem in the two short sides of the fabric rectangle.

3 Place the fabric rectangle right side down on a flat work surface. Center the pillow on top of the fabric.

4 Take each side of the fabric and fold them in towards the center of the pillow until the ends overlap in the center. Use straight pins to pin the unhemmed edges of the fabric together.

5 Remove the pillow, leaving the pins in place.

6 Using a 1-inch (2.5 cm) seam allowance, sew down each pinned edge.

7 Turn the pillow cover right side out and press it flat.

8 Reinsert the pillow inside the pillow cover, then the short, hemmed edges under the long, sewn edge.

MATERIALS

One piece of fabric for each pillow—see *Determining the Amount of Fabric* below

Iron-on seam tape

TOOLS

Tape measure

Scissors

Iron and ironing board

Straight pins

COMFORTER TRIM

Here's a super-quick fix for changing the look of your everyday comforter—simply add a fabric trim to the top. Then, when you turn down the comforter, the trim splashes a new wave of color across your entire bed!

MATERIALS

1 fabric rectangle*

Iron-on seam tape

A length of adhesive-backed hook-and-loop tape—the same measurement as the width of your comforter (optional)

TOOLS

Scissors

Iron and ironing board

Glue gun and glue sticks (optional)

* You want the length of the rectangle to be the measurement of your comforter plus 2 inches (5 cm), and the width of the rectangle to be 28 inches (71 cm).

INSTRUCTIONS

1 Cut a fabric rectangle from your chosen fabric to the measurements determined by the width of your comforter.

2 Use iron-on seam tape to make a 1-inch (2.5 cm) hem along the two side (selvage) edges of the fabric rectangle.

3 Use iron-on seam tape to make a 1-inch (2.5 cm) hem along the two remaining raw edges of the fabric rectangle.

4 Fold the fabric rectangle lengthwise, wrong sides together.

5 Use iron-on seam tape to attach the three sides of the folded fabric rectangle together.

6 Place the finished trim over the top of your comforter, allowing approximately 5 inches (12.5 cm) to extend past the top of the comforter. Use hot glue or a length of adhesive-backed hook-and-loop tape to attach the trim piece to the comforter.

FABRIC BED-TRAY LINER

Change the look of a bed tray as often as you like by changing the fabric liner. This one is made from fabric that coordinates with the room, but you can also select seasonal fabrics for different looks throughout the year.

MATERIALS

Heavy-duty poster board—a piece the size of your tray

1 piece of fabric the size of your tray plus a 1-inch (2.5 cm) allowance on all four sides

TOOLS

Sharp utility knife

Metal straightedge

Scissors

Glue gun and glue sticks

INSTRUCTIONS

1 From the heavy-duty poster board, use a sharp utility knife and a metal straightedge or ruler to cut a rectangle the size of the inside eating surface of your bed tray.

2 From the fabric, cut a piece that is the same size as the rectangle of poster board, plus a 1-inch (2.5 cm) allowance on all four sides.

3 Place the fabric rectangle right side down on a flat work surface and center the poster board panel on top of it. Clip all four corners of the fabric, and fold the 1-inch (2.5 cm) allowance over the edges of the poster board. Use hot glue to attach the fabric allowance to the backside of the poster board.

4 Place the finished liner on the bed tray, securing the liner to the tray with hot glue.

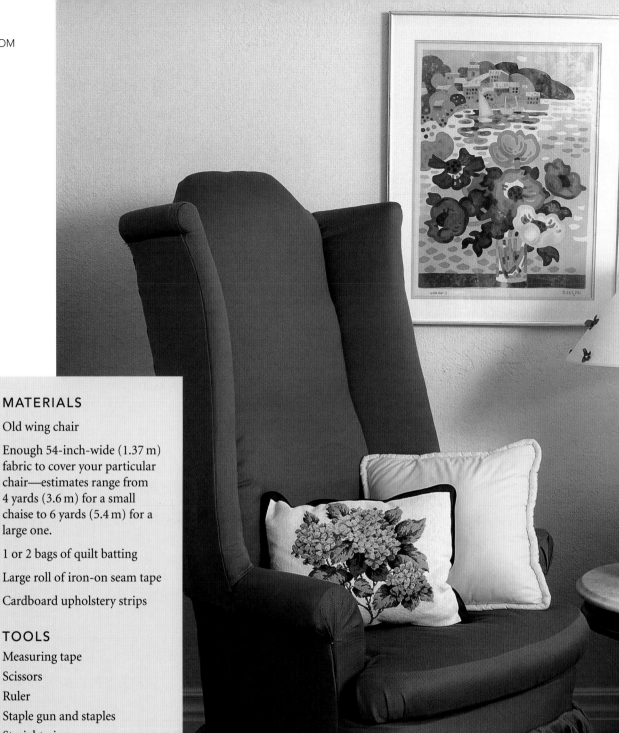

MATERIALS

Old wing chair

Enough 54-inch-wide (1.37 m) fabric to cover your particular chair—estimates range from 4 yards (3.6 m) for a small chaise to 6 yards (5.4 m) for a large one.

1 or 2 bags of quilt batting

Large roll of iron-on seam tape

Cardboard upholstery strips

TOOLS

Measuring tape

Scissors

Ruler

Staple gun and staples

Straight pins

Pencil

Glue gun and glue sticks

Craft paper

Iron and ironing Board

WING CHAIR

When we found this wing chair at an estate sale, the old upholstery had seen better days. Since the frame was sturdy, we decided to give it a new home, and a new lease on life, by reupholstering it. Using a glue gun and staple gun, we found it is possible to perform a "chair lift" for a very reasonable cost.

INSTRUCTIONS

Surveying the Project

To upholster a piece of furniture, you must logically think through the project before you begin. The trick is to think in layers. The previous upholstery job will give you the answer. Survey your piece to determine how the upholstery was done. Also take note of any "dips" or "swaybacks" in the chair, and fill these depressions by adding quilt batting as needed as you work. You want to make sure the fabric is always oriented in the proper direction. For example, if you are using a floral fabric, make sure that the flower motif is right-side-up on the finished chair. Don't be intimidated by the process. If you work slowly and thoughtfully, you'll be proud of your finished job.

Covering the Arms and Back

1 To begin, remove the chair cushion and set it aside. Cover the inside of the chair arms first. Using the chair as a pattern, cut a piece of fabric large enough to cover the inside of the arm and to wrap around its underside. As a margin for error and for attaching the fabric to the frame, plan for a 2- to 3-inch (5 to 7.5 cm) allowance on your cut piece. Staple

the fabric tightly to the frame first at the bottom inside of the arm. Then staple the center bottom of the fabric to the center of the frame. Continue to staple, working out toward the edges in both directions, easing the fabric around the front of the arm.

2 Next, bring the top edge of the fabric over the top of the arm, and staple it to the chair frame under the arm, as shown in figure 1. Add quilt batting to the arm as necessary. Again begin stapling in the center of the underarm, and work out in both directions. Repeat to cover the opposite chair arm.

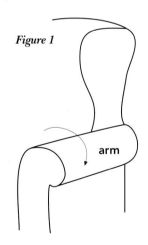

Figure 1

arm

3 Next, cover the wings of the chair, using the same procedure for covering the arms.

Covering the Under Seat and Lower Front

1 Cut a piece of fabric the size of the front of the chair and the under seat (the portion of the chair under the cushion). As a margin for error, plan for a 3-inch (7.5 cm) allowance.

2 Lay the fabric piece over the under seat. Using the eraser end of a pencil, push the fabric into the spaces between the under seat, arms, and back. Attach the fabric to the center back of the under seat. If you can reach the chair frame at that point, staple the fabric in place. Otherwise use hot glue. Smooth the fabric over the under seat, toward the center of the chair front. Staple the fabric to the lower edge of the chair front.

3 Repeat the procedure to attach the remaining fabric to the under seat and chair front, working out from the center toward the edges. When you reach the point where the chair front meets the outer edge of the arm, staple the fabric to the chair frame just past that point.

Covering the Wings

1 Make a paper pattern for the wings. Pin a piece of craft paper to the back of a wing, and cut it to fit properly. It should just cover the back of the wing, and wrap under the arm extension. When the pattern is perfect, remove it from the chair, and cut a piece of fabric to that size, adding a 2-inch (5 cm) allowance around all the edges.

2 Use an iron to press a 2-inch (5 cm) hem along the top and front edges of your fabric piece (in that order), as shown in figure 2.

Figure 2

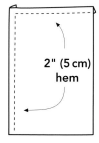

2" (5 cm) hem

3 Open the pressed side hem of the fabric, and place the top corner, with the right side of the fabric toward the chair, at the top front corner of the wing. Use a straight pin to hold it in place. The hem should be against the chair, and the rest of the fabric should be in front of the chair, as shown in figure 3. Beginning at the wing's front corner, match the fold in the hem to the front edge of the wing back. Again use straight pins to hold the fabric in place. Place cardboard upholstery strips along the pressed hem line, and staple through the cardboard and fabric into the chair

frame, covering the raw edges of the previous fabric on the front of the wing. Smooth the fabric, and work down the wing toward the bottom.

4 Making sure the top hem is flat, pull the fabric across the top of the wing to the back of the chair and staple it to the chair frame. Continue working down the back of the wing, smoothing the fabric and stapling it to the chair frame on the back of the chair. Using a hot glue gun, glue the top hem in place across the top of the wing.

Covering the Underarm and Chair Back

1 Cut a paper pattern for the underarm section of the chair, and the chair back. From the patterns, cut two pieces of fabric for the underarm section, and one for the back, adding a 2-inch (5 cm) allowance on all sides of each piece.

2 Use an iron to press a 2-inch (5 cm) hem along the top and front edges of your fabric piece.

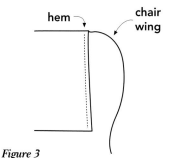

hem   chair wing

Figure 3

3 Repeat steps 3 and 4 under *Covering the Wings* to cover both underarm sections.

Covering the Back

1 Cut a paper pattern the exact size of the chair back. Use the paper pattern to cut a piece of fabric for the back, adding a 2-inch (5 cm) allowance on all sides.

2 Use iron-on seam tape to make a 2-inch (5 cm) hem along both sides of the back fabric. Then use an iron to press a 2-inch (5 cm) hem along the top edge of your fabric piece.

3 Open up the pressed top hem of the fabric, and place the top corner, with the right sides of the fabric toward the chair, at the top front corner of the wing. Use a straight pin to hold it in place. The hem should be against the back of the chair, and the rest of the fabric should be flipped over the front of the chair.

4 Beginning at the center of the back, match the fold in the hem to the top edge of the back. Use straight pins to hold the fabric in place. Place cardboard upholstery strips along the pressed hem line, and staple through the cardboard and fabric into the chair frame, covering the raw edges of the previous fabric on the front of the chair back. Smooth the fabric, and work toward both sides.

5 Working from the top down and alternating sides, attach the side edges of the back fabric to the chair, using straight pins to hold them in place until the glue dries. Smooth the fabric from top to bottom, and staple the back to the chair frame.

Adding the Skirt

1 The skirt is made from gathered panels of 54-inch-wide (1.37 m) fabric. To determine the length of each panel, measure the distance from the just above the staples at the front of the chair to the floor, double that measurement and add 1 inch (2.5 cm). To determine the total width of the panels you will need, measure entirely around the chair, then multiply that number by two. Cut enough panels to satisfy these measurements. If you have access to a sewing machine, seam the panels together. If you don't have a machine, you will need to hem both sides of each panel. We made our skirt using a solid fabric. If you are using a pattern, it needs to be matched across the skirt, and requires more fabric than a solid. If you are not familiar with the term "drop", please read that section on page 10 in *Tips and Techniques* before cutting the panel.

2 Use iron-on seam tape to make a 1-inch (2.5 cm) hem along the two selvage (side) edges of a skirt panel. Then fold the hemmed panel lengthwise, wrong sides together.

3 Lay the folded panel on a flat work surface. Gently gather the two top raw edges of the panel with your hands, until the panel width measures approximately 27 inches (68.5 cm) across the top, keeping the raw edges as straight and even as possible. Secure the gathers, using hot glue. Since only ½ inch (1.3 cm) of the gathered top will be hidden, try to keep the glue within that area. Repeat steps 2 and 3 to hem and gather the remaining skirt panels.

4 Place the chair on the work surface so that the front is facing the work surface. Begin at the center back of the chair and place a skirt panel over the staples in the lower edge of the chair so that the gathered raw edges are flush with the lower edge of the chair back. Place a cardboard upholstery strip over the 1-inch (2.5 cm) extension of the skirt panel so that the bottom of the strip is flush with the lower edge of the chair, as shown in figure 4. Staple through the cardboard strip and skirt panel into the chair frame. Use enough staples to hold the cardboard strips securely.

Figure 4

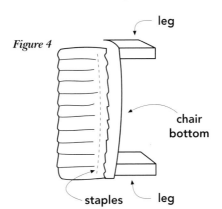

leg

chair
bottom

staples   leg

5 Continue adding fabric panels, each time overlapping the previous panel by 1 inch (2.5 cm). Once the skirt is applied, turn the chair over and adjust the gathers.

Covering the Cushion

1 Cut a piece of fabric to the top and side dimensions of your seat cushion, adding a 3-inch (7.5 cm) allowance on all sides.

2 Temporarily pin the fabric to the seat cushion, then pull the fabric over the sides of the cushion to the opposite sides, easing the fabric over the edges, and smoothing as much as possible. Glue the fabric in place on the bottom of the cushion. If you have inside curves on your cushion, you will need to clip the fabric frequently to make it smoothly round the curve. We left our clips exposed since they would not be seen when the cushion is in place. However, if this bothers you, simply cut a length of fabric the width of the cushion side, plus a 2-inch (5 cm) allowance for hemming, hem with iron-on seam tape, then glue it around all sides of the cushion.

3 Replace the cushion on the completed chair.

FLOWERED LAMP AND LAMPSHADE

Give any old lamp a flowered springtime look with some fabric, a few silk flowers, and some paper butterflies.

INSTRUCTIONS

Covering the Lamp

1 Place the fabric right side down on your work surface. Center the lamp on top of the fabric, and trace around the base with a pencil.

2 Draw a straight line on the fabric from where the lamp cord emerges from the side of the lamp, to the edge of the fabric.

3 Remove the lamp from the fabric, and cut the fabric along the straight line that you drew (do not cut around the circle of the lamp base).

4 With wrong sides together, fold the fabric in approximately ½ inch (1.3 cm) on both sides of the cut and press in place. Secure the fabric with hot glue.

5 The next step is easier if you can enlist the assistance of a helper. Center the lamp base on the fabric over the tracing of the base, making sure the lamp cord matches the hemmed slit in the fabric. Gather all the sides of the fabric around the top of the lamp and tie a string or lightweight wire very tightly around the fabric.

Finishing

1 Adjust the fabric gathers until they are evenly spaced around the entire lamp.

2 Fold the excess fabric at the top of the lamp back over itself to the center of the lamp to form a "puff" at the top of the lamp. Glue the fabric in place.

3 Glue individual flowers to the lampshade, spacing them randomly. Then glue six to eight butterflies to the lampshade among the flowers.

4 Tie a satin cord around the top of the lamp to cover the string or wire, tying the ends of the cord into a bow.

MATERIALS

1½ yards (1.37 m) of 54-inch-wide (1.37 m) fabric*

Old lamp no larger than 50 inches (1.25 m) measuring from the top of the lamp base, across the bottom of the base, and back up to the opposite side of the top

String or lightweight wire

A few individual silk flowers—we chose violets

6 or 8 paper or silk butterflies

Satin cord

TOOLS

Measuring tape

Flat work surface

Pencil

Ruler

Scissors

Glue gun and glue sticks

We chose a large floral pattern to coordinate with our room You need a fairly lightweight fabric for this project to form the "puff" at the top of the lamp.

BALLOON CURTAINS

This balloon shade look-alike requires no sewing, and mimics the appearance of much more expensive window treatments. It's the perfect addition to a frilly bedroom or bath.

INSTRUCTIONS

Determining the Amount of Fabric

To cover a 36-inch-wide (.9 m) window that is 35 inches (.89 m) long, we used two lengths of 54-inch-wide (1.37 m) fabric, each measuring 64 inches (1.6 m) long. If your window is larger than that, extra fabric will be required. If your window is smaller than that, cut the fabric proportionally. We used a medium-weight, small floral print.

Making the Curtains

1 Cut two fabric panels to the proper measurements for your window.

2 Use iron-on seam tape to make a 1-inch (2.5 cm) hem in both selvage (side) edges of the fabric panels.

3 Use iron-on seam tape to make a 1-inch (2.5 cm) hem in both remaining edges of the fabric panels.

4 Place one fabric panel right side down on a flat surface. Measure and mark a line across the width of the fabric that is 17 inches (42.5 cm) from one end. Mark a second line across the width of the fabric that is 22 inches (56 cm) from the first, as shown in figure 1.

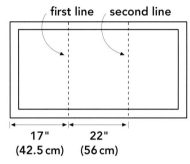

first line   second line

17"   22"
(42.5 cm)   (56 cm)

Figure 1

5 To make a pocket for the curtain rod, fold the fabric along the first line, then measure 1 inch (2.5 cm) down from both sides of that fold line. Fold the fabric at the 1-inch (2.5 cm) line, pressing it toward the hem above the first mark as shown in figure 2. Use iron-on seam tape on the edge of the fold to attach the fold to the fabric. Make sure you leave enough room in the pocket for passing the tension rod through it.

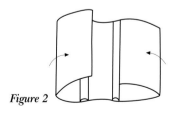

Figure 2

6 Repeat the procedure in step 5 on the second line you marked in step 4.

7 Lay the fabric panel right side down on a flat work surface. Take the hem that is just above the first mark and fold it back toward the pocket you made in step 5. Use hot glue to attach the bottom of the hem to the base of the pocket.

8 Take the bottom hem that is below the second mark, and fold it toward the base of the second pocket made in step 6. Use hot glue to attach the bottom hem along the base of the second pocket.

9 Repeat steps 4 through 8, using the remaining panel.

10 Insert a tension rod through each of the pockets in both panels, and hang them inside the window frame. The first pocket should be placed at the topmost point of the window. We placed the second tension rod approximately 15 inches (37.5 cm) from the top of the window. Adjust the fabric to fluff the "balloons."

MATERIALS

54-inch-wide (1.37 m) fabric—see *Determining the Amount of Fabric* below

Iron-on seam tape

2 tension rods

TOOLS

Scissors

Flat work surface

Iron and ironing board

RUFFLE-SKIRTED SIDE TABLE

Transform that garage-sale end table or night stand into a charming bedroom table with the addition of a fabric top and ruffled skirt. We love the look, and get many compliments on our "new" furniture.

MATERIALS

Two coordinating 54-inch-wide (1.37 m) fabrics—see *Determining the Amount of Fabric* below

Quilt batting

Iron-on seam tape

Cardboard upholstery strips*

TOOLS

Measuring tape

Scissors

Glue gun and glue sticks

Staple gun and staples

Iron and ironing board

* You can purchase these at most upholstery shops, or you can make your own by cutting poster board into ½-inch (1.3 cm) strips using a utility knife and a metal straight-edge—just make sure that at least one side of the strip is exactly straight.

INSTRUCTIONS

Determining the Amount of Fabric

For the ruffle, you'll need several fabric panels. The number of panels and their length will depend upon the size of table you are covering. Allowing for a 1-inch (2.5 cm) overlap on each side, each gathered panel will cover approximately 22 linear inches (56 cm). To find the number of panels you'll need, measure the circumference of your furniture, then divide by 22 (56). To determine the length of each panel, measure the distance from the floor to just under the top of your table, double that measurement, then add 2 inches (5 cm) to that measurement. We used a medium-weight large floral fabric for our ruffle.

To cover the top, you'll use a coordinating fabric (we used a small floral companion print). To determine the amount of fabric you need for the top, measure the length and width of your furniture top. To that measurement, add a 4-inch (10 cm) allowance on all four sides.

Covering the Top

1 Measure the length and width of your table top. To that measurement, add a 4-inch (10 cm) allowance on all four sides. Cut a piece of quilt batting to these dimensions.

2 Center the quilt batting over the top. Use the hot glue to temporarily secure it to the top.

3 Cut a piece of fabric to the dimensions of your top determined in step 1 (Remember to add the 4-inch [10 cm] allowance on all four sides.)

4 Center the fabric over the quilt batting, and staple it to the side of the furniture just under the top. Use enough staples to hold the fabric evenly and securely in place. You can minimize the number of wrinkles if you start by stapling the center of one long side, then the center of the opposite long side. Then work your way out toward the ends, smoothing the fabric as you go. Next, staple the center of each of the ends, and again work your way out toward the corners. Ease the fabric over the corners, eliminating as many wrinkles as possible.

Adding the Ruffled Skirt

1 Cut a skirt panel from your chosen fabric to the measurements determined by your table—see *Determining the Amount of Fabric* above.

2 Use iron-on seam tape to make a 1-inch (2.5 cm) hem along the two selvage (side) edges of the skirt panel, as shown in figure 1.

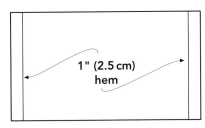

Figure 1

3 Fold the hemmed panel lengthwise with wrong sides together. Lay the folded panel on a flat work surface. Gently gather the two top raw edges of the panel with your hands, until the panel width mea-sures approximately 24 inches (61 cm)

across the top. Try to keep the raw edges as straight and even as possible. Secure the gathers, using hot glue.

4 Turn the table upside down. (You may want to cover your surface to protect the already covered top). Beginning at the back of the table, place a skirt panel over the upside-down top with the gathered raw edges extending 1 inch (2.5 cm) over the side of the furniture. Place a cardboard upholstery strip over the 1-inch (2.5 cm) extension of the skirt panel so that the bottom of the strip is flush with the underside of the furniture top, as shown in figure 2.

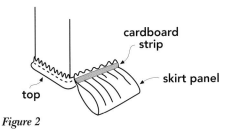

cardboard strip

skirt panel

top

Figure 2

5 Staple through the cardboard and skirt panel into the side of the furniture. Use enough staples to hold the cardboard strip securely.

6 Continue attaching fabric panels and cardboard strips, overlapping the previous panel by 1 inch (2.5 cm) each time.

7 When the entire furniture piece is covered, turn it right side up and adjust the gathers in the skirt.

GUEST BATH

This room proves that a few easy touches can beautifully transform a room. The shower curtain is easy to make and hang. The fabric pictures instantly coordinate the room, while the table drape handsomely brightens a small corner. We chose a fern print because we wanted to give this small room a fresh, outdoor look.

FABRIC PICTURES

If you've been to a fabric store lately, you already know that there are hundreds of fabric patterns that are organized in squares or rectangles. We used such a pattern to create unique pictures for our bathroom walls.

MATERIALS

Fabric in a square pattern—we used the same fabric as our shower curtain*

1 canvas stretcher for each picture—these are available at frame shops and art supply stores, and can be sized to fit your fabric design

Masking tape

1 picture hanger for each of the pictures

TOOLS

Scissors

Flat work surface

Staple gun and staples

*Buy enough fabric to make the number of pictures you want. In our case, just over ½ yard (.45 m) was enough to make four pictures.

INSTRUCTIONS

1 Cut out the fabric square you wish to frame, leaving approximately a 2 or 3 inch (5 or 7.5 cm) allowance on all sides of the design.

2 Place the assembled canvas stretcher on a flat work surface. Center the fabric picture over the stretcher and adjust it until the picture is square horizontally and vertically. Use masking tape to hold it in place temporarily.

3 Turn the entire assembly upside down so the fabric picture is facing the work surface. Use a staple gun to attach the edges of the fabric to the back of the canvas stretcher. Use enough staples to hold the fabric evenly and securely in place. You can minimize the number of wrinkles if you start by stapling the center of one long side and the center of the opposite long side. Then work your way out toward the ends, smoothing the fabric as you go. Next, staple the center of each of the ends, and again

work your way out toward the corners. Neatly fold the fabric over the corners, eliminating as many wrinkles as possible.

4 Cut off any excess fabric—you want the picture to lie as flat as possible against the wall. Install a picture hanger at the top back of the canvas stretcher.

SHOWER CURTAIN

Turn your bathroom into a designer showcase with the addition of a fabric shower curtain that you make yourself. You can easily attach it to the shower rod with the matching fabric ties.

MATERIALS

5 yards (4.6 m) of 54-inch-wide (1.37 m) medium-weight fabric*

18 extra-large grommets

Large roll of iron-on seam tape

2 plastic shower-curtain liners

TOOLS

Tape measure

Scissors

Iron and ironing board

Grommet tool

Hammer

*Check the repeat of your fabric. For our shower curtain as shown, we purchased extra yardage to ensure that the squares on the finished panels would be at the same height across both curtains. With the leftover fabric, we made the fabric ties.

INSTRUCTIONS

Making the Panels

1 Cut a panel from the fabric that is 75 inches (1.8 m) long.

2 Use iron-on seam tape to mak a ½-inch (1.3 cm) hem in each of the selvage sides of the curtain panel.

3 Use iron-on seam tape to make a 2-inch (5 cm) hem in what will be the top of the curtain panel.

4 Use iron-on seam tape to make a 1-inch (2.5 cm) hem in what will be the bottom of the curtain panel.

5 Using the holes in a plastic shower liner as your guide, use the grommet tool to insert nine extra-large grommets in the top of the curtain panel.

6 Repeat steps 1 through 5 to make a second curtain panel.

Finishing the Curtain

1 Cut 16 fabric ties, each measuring 22 x 5½ inches (56 x 13.8 cm).

2 Use iron-on seam tape to make a 1-inch (2.5 cm) hem in each short end of the tie.

3 Use iron-on seam tape to make a 1-inch (2.5 cm) hem along one long edge of the tie.

4 Use iron-on seam tape to make a 1½-inch (3.8 cm) hem along the opposite long edge of the tie.

5 Fold the 1-inch (2.5 cm) hemmed edge over the 1½-inch (3.8 cm) hem until the tie measures 2 inches wide (5 cm). Press in place.

6 Repeat steps 2 through 5, using the remaining 15 fabric ties.

7 To hang the curtains, insert a fabric tie through each grommet hole in the curtain, then tie them in a knot on top of the shower rod. Overlap the first two grommet holes in the second curtain over the last two grommet holes in the first curtain. As you did for the curtains, overlap the two liners behind the curtains.

TABLE DRAPE

This fringed table drape can go anywhere, but we used it to add some drama to our guest bathroom.

MATERIALS

54-inch-wide (1.37 m) fabric—see Determining the Amount of Fabric below

Old table

Fringe in a coordinating color—measure the outer edge of the completed table drape to determine how much you need

Iron-on seam tape

TOOLS

Measuring tape

Scissors

Flat work surface

Iron and ironing board

Glue gun and glue sticks

INSTRUCTIONS

Determining the Amount of Fabric

Unless you want to seam two widths of fabric together, you are limited in the size table you can cover. Measure your table from the floor at the front, over the top of the table, and down the back to the floor again. Then measure from one side at the floor, over the top, and back down the other side to the floor again. If one of these measurements is 53 inches (1.3 m) or less, you can cover that table with one 54-inch (1.37 m) width of fabric. The remaining measurement will tell you what length of fabric you will need.

Draping the Table

1 Place the length of fabric over the table, making sure that it is straight across the top, and hangs evenly on all four sides.

2 Use a pencil or piece of marking chalk to mark along the bottom of the fabric drape where it meets the floor.

3 Remove the drape from the table and cut along the marked line. If you are adding a wide fringe, cut the fabric drape a bit shorter, allowing for a ½-inch (1.3 cm) deep hem.

4 Use iron-on seam tape to make a ½-inch (1.3 cm) hem on all four sides of the fabric drape.

5 Use a glue gun to attach the fringe over the hem on all sides of the drape.

BEDROOM OFFICE

Our bedroom office gives us the flexibility of a multi-purpose living space. The earth tones in an ethnic theme create a room that is both restful and conducive to work. We solved the problem of old, unattractive closet doors by simply covering them with fabric. You'll be surprised to find that the bedcover requires no sewing. The desktop, headboard, and shelf all serve practical purposes while helping to coordinating the room.

FABRIC-COVERED CLOSET DOORS

Our old house has wooden sliding doors on the bedroom closets. Since the doors were in bad shape, we thought about replacing them. The door size was difficult to find, making replacement an expensive custom order. Instead, we decided to see what they would look like covered in fabric. Now they serve as a place to pin posters, and are an attractive solution to a pesky problem.

MATERIALS

2 pieces of fabric in your choice of colors*

TOOLS

Scissors

Staple gun and staples

* To prevent raveling, we suggest that you choose a heavy-weight fabric with a backing.

INSTRUCTIONS

1 Each piece of fabric needs to be large enough to cover the front and the four edges of each door. Measure your door front and edges. To that measurement add a 1-inch (2.5 cm) allowance on all four sides. Cut two pieces of fabric to this measurement.

2 Remove the old sliding doors by lifting them out of their track. Old doors can be very heavy, so seek assistance if needed.

3 Place the fabric right side down on a flat work surface. Center the door over the top of the fabric, wrong side down, and wrap the edges of the fabric over the top edge of the door, and staple it in place. You can minimize the number of wrinkles if you first attach the center of one side, then the center of the opposite side. Then work your way out toward the corners. Pull the fabric tightly as you go. Attach the center of the remaining sides, and again work your way toward the corners. Be generous with the staples; use enough to keep the fabric from puckering along the sides. Tuck the corners in neatly and uniformly (right-angle "hospital" corners are ideal), then staple the fabric in place.

4 Replace the covered doors in their track.

BEDCOVER

Can't find a bedspread or comforter you like? Or if you can—can you afford it? Here's a simple solution. Make your own for a custom look, at a fraction of the price.

INSTRUCTIONS

Determining the Amount of Fabric

For the top of the bedcover you will need 2½ yards (2.2 m) of 54-inch-wide (1.37 m) fabric. For the sides you will need 7½ yards (6.8 m) of 54-inch-wide (1.37 m) fabric. If you do not want to use braid or belting for your trim, you can make your own from fabric. To do so, you will need an additional 2½ yards (2.2 m) of coordinating fabric, or you can use the fabric you will have left over from making the sides.

Constructing the Sides and Top

1 Make the sides first. If the fabric's selvage is not attractive, use iron-on seam tape to make a 1-inch (2.5 cm) hem in the selvage side that will be against the floor. Beginning at the head of the bed, position the fabric on the bed so that the width hangs almost to the floor, and the excess remains on top of the bed. As you work, use straight pins to pin the fabric in place temporarily. Continue positioning the fabric in this manner, down one side of the bed, across the foot of the bed, and up the opposite side toward the head again. At each of the corners of the foot of the bed, add an inverted pleat. Each side of the pleat should measure 6 inches (15 cm) wide.

2 Make the top. Place the second fabric over the top of the bed, positioning it over the excess side fabric. Smooth the top fabric as much as possible. Use a pencil to trace the outline of the top of the bedcover onto the sides.

3 Remove the excess fabric from the sides. First, remove the top fabric. Then, on all sides, cut 2 inches (5 cm) inside the line of the traced top. (Figure the 2 inches (5 cm) from the line toward the center of the bed.)

4 Use a glue gun and hot glue to secure the folds of the pleats together that are on each corner at the foot of the bed.

5 Replace the top fabric and smooth it out. Use hot glue to attach the top to the sides, working from the center of the foot of the bed, up both sides toward the head of the bed. Remove the straight pins as you work.

Adding the Trim (optional)

Glue purchased braid or belting over the joining of the top and sides. Starting at the head, work from one side, across the foot, and back up to the opposite side of the head.

If you want to make your own trim, cut a 5½-inch-wide (13.8 cm) strip from the excess side fabric that measures the entire length of the fabric. Use iron-on seam tape to make a 1-inch (2.5 cm) hem in each short end of the strip. Then use the iron-on seam tape to make a 1-inch (2.5 cm) hem along one long edge of the strip. Along the opposite long end, use the iron to press in a 1½-inch (3.8 cm) hem.

Fold the strip until it measures 2 inches (5 cm) wide with the 1-inch (2.5 cm) seamed edge over the 1½-inch (3.8 cm) pressed edge. Use hot glue to glue the long edges together. Then attach the trim to the bedcover.

MATERIALS*

Two coordinating 54-inch-wide (1.37 m) fabrics—see *Determining the Amount of Fabric below* **

Iron-on seam tape

Woven braid or belting, in a coordinated color (optional)

TOOLS

Measuring tape
Scissors
Iron and ironing board
Glue gun and glue sticks

*The materials specified will make a bedcover for a queen-size bed. If you have a king-size bed, you will need twice the amount of fabric for the top of the bed-cover, and will have to seam two widths together. For the sides, you will need 1extra yard (.9 m) of fabric.

**For best results, use a heavy-weight upholstery fabric that will not ravel easily. We chose a fabric with a woven selvage so that we did not have to hem it.

MATERIALS*

1 piece of 4-inch (10 cm) foam, measuring 24 by 56 inches (61 x 142 cm)

1 piece of heavyweight fabric measuring 40 by 72 inches (101.5 x 180 cm)—to prevent raveling, we chose an upholstery fabric with a backing

Adhesive-backed hook-and-loop tape, 54 inches (1.37 m)

TOOLS

Electric knife (if you are cutting the foam yourself)

Scissors

Hot glue gun and glue sticks

Our materials list is specifically for a queen-size bed. If you have a larger or smaller bed, you can alter the length of the foam and the fabric.

PADDED HEADBOARD

If your bedroom lacks a coordinated look, this quick project should solve your problems. The headboard is made from 4-inch (10 cm) foam and a fabric covering.

INSTRUCTIONS

1 Cut the 4-inch (10 cm) foam to 24 by 56 inches (61 x 142 cm). If you are cutting it yourself, an electric knife works best. However, most stores that sell foam will cut it for you.

2 Cut a piece of fabric measuring 40 by 72 inches (101.5 x 180 cm).

3 Place the fabric right side down on a flat work surface. Center the foam over the top of the fabric, and wrap the edges of the fabric over the top edge of the foam, using the hot glue to attach it in place. You can minimize the number of wrinkles if you first attach the center of one side, then the center of the opposite side, then work your way out toward the corners. Smooth the fabric as you go. Attach the center of the remaining sides, and again work your way toward the corners. Be generous with the glue; use enough to keep the fabric from puckering along the sides. Tuck the corners in neatly and uniformly (right-angle "hospital" corners are ideal), then glue the fabric in place.

4 Remove one side of the paper backing from the 54-inch-long (1.37 m) piece of hook- and-loop tape. Attach the tape to the center top back of the finished headboard. Remove the remaining paper backing, and attach the other side of the hook-and-loop tape to the wall, centering it over your bed.

MOCK SHADE

Since this window treatment covers the window, you can use it to screen out a less than desirable view—all you need is a length of fabric and a tension rod.

INSTRUCTIONS

1 Cut a piece of fabric to the dimensions needed for your window.

2 Use iron-on seam tape to make a ½-inch (1.3 cm) hem along one of the long sides of the fabric rectangle.

3 Use iron-on seam tape to make a ½-inch (1.3 cm) hem along the opposite long side of the rectangle.

4 Use iron-on seam tape to make a 1-inch (2.5 cm) hem in one of the short sides of the rectangle. Note: We were able to pull threads from the fabric to make a fringed edge.

5 Hang the completed shade over a tension rod.

MATERIALS

1 piece of fabric that is 1 inch (2.5 cm) wider than the width of your window, and double the length of the portion of the window you wish to cover*

Iron-on seam tape

Drapery tension rod

TOOLS

Tape measure

Scissors

Iron and ironing board

You want to select a fabric that will hold its shape. We chose a heavyweight upholstery fabric with a backing.

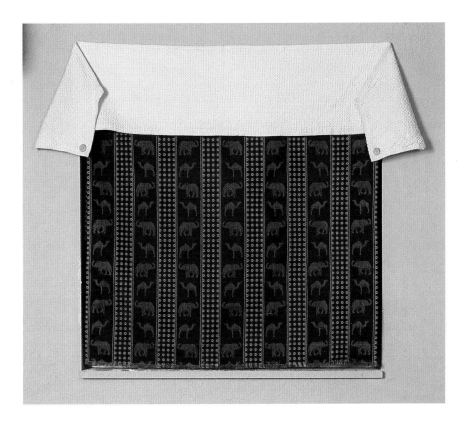

QUICK-FIX TABLE-RUNNER VALANCE

If you are looking for an instant valance, purchase a table runner. They are inexpensive and come in many different styles and patterns. Their length gives you enough extra fabric for easily spanning a window. The ends of the runners are usually finished with decorative touches, such as tassels and buttons, giving you an instant designer look. To hang the valance, all you need to do is simply center it across the top of your window and nail it in place!

MATERIALS

Old or new fan

½-yard (.45 m) of fabric in a color of your choice*

Craft paper

Spray adhesive

TOOLS

Old newspapers

Pencil

Scissors

Craft knife

*We suggest using a heavyweight upholstery fabric with a backing that won't allow it to ravel. If you are using a fabric with a distinctive repeat, make certain that you allow enough extra fabric for placing each of the fan blades on the same portion of the design.

FABRIC-COVERED CEILING FAN

Hate those boring white fan blades? You can create a designer look in no time on an old or new ceiling fan, using a small amount of fabric and some spray adhesive.

INSTRUCTIONS

Removing the Fan Blades

NOTE: If you are working with a new fan that is not assembled, go directly to *Adding the Fabric*.

1 Remove all of the fan blades from the fan by unscrewing them where the arm of the blade meets the body of the fan.

2 Remove the blades from the arm assemblies.

3 Clean the fan blades with soap and water, and allow them to dry thoroughly.

Adding the Fabric

1 Place one fan blade on a piece of craft paper. Use a pencil to trace the outline of the blade.

2 Use the scissors to cut out the paper pattern of the blade, cutting ⅛-inch (.3 cm) inside the traced lines.

3 Lay the paper pattern on the fabric. If you are using a fabric with a distinctive repeat, make certain that you place the pattern on the same portion of the design for each of the fan blades. Pin the pattern in place, then cut around the pattern. Repeat, to cut a piece of fabric for each of the fan blades.

4 Place the fabric pieces right side down on newspapers, and spray the wrong side of each fabric piece with spray adhesive. Follow the manufacturer's directions to attach the fabric to the fan blade—some products require spraying both surfaces before joining. Be sure to apply the fabric to the correct side of the fan blade every time, and to keep the fabric absolutely smooth across the entire blade.

5 Use a craft knife to poke a hole through the fabric where the screws for the arm assembly will be positioned.

6 Attach the arm to the fan blade by inserting screws through the arm and into the fan blade.

7 Attach each of the blade assemblies to the fan body, using screws.

BED PILLOW ROLL

This classic bedroom accessory will give an elegantly different look to any bed. The base is a cardboard fabric tube, making the project fast and easy to put together.

MATERIALS

54-inch-long (1.37 m) cardboard tube—this is used for rolling fabric, and most fabric stores will have a supply

1 piece of 2-inch (5 cm) foam measuring 54 by 26 inches (137 x 66 cm)

5 yards (4.6 m) of string

1 bag of quilt batting

2 yards (1.8 m) of 54-inch-wide (1.37 m) medium-weight fabric—we chose an animal print to coordinate with our room

Iron-on seam tape

2 rubber bands

2 curtain tiebacks with tassels attached, in a color to coordinate with your fabric

TOOLS

Electric knife (if you are cutting the foam yourself)

Scissors

Glue gun and glue sticks

Iron

Ironing board

INSTRUCTIONS

1 Cut the 2-inch (5 cm) foam to 54 by 26 inches (137 x 66 cm). If you are cutting it yourself, an electric knife works best. However, most stores that sell foam will cut it for you.

2 Wrap the foam around the cardboard tube. As you wrap, check to make sure the long edges of the foam come together neatly. If necessary, trim the foam, then use hot glue to attach it to the cardboard tube. After gluing, use the string to hold the foam in place by tying lengths of string around it in five or six places along its length.

3 To even out your cylinder, wrap layers of quilt batting around the foam over the depressions made by the tied string.

4 Measure the circumference and length of your batting-wrapped cylinder. To those measurements, add 6 inches (15 cm) to the circumference and 20 inches (50 cm) to the length. Cut a piece of fabric to those dimensions.

5 Use iron-on seam tape to make a 1-inch (2.5 cm) hem along the two long edges of your fabric.

6 Use iron-on seam tape to make a 5-inch (12.5 cm) hem along the two short edges of your fabric.

7 Center the wrapped pillow form along one long edge of your fabric, and roll the fabric over the form. Secure the final edge with hot glue.

8 Gather the ends of the pillow with your hands, and tie a rubber band close to each end of the pillow. Tie a curtain tieback (with attached tassel) over the rubber band.

FABRIC DESKTOP

Nothing could be easier than this fabric-covered desktop. In just an hour or two you can transform a weather-beaten desk into a distinctive piece of furniture. We added a piece of clear plastic sheeting to keep it looking fresh and clean.

MATERIALS

54-inch-wide (1.37 m) fabric in a color of your choice*

Clear plastic sheeting or glass (optional)

TOOLS

Tape measure

Scissors

Staple gun and staples

We chose a heavyweight uphol-stery fabric to coordinate with the rest of our room.

INSTRUCTIONS

1 Measure your desktop. To that measurement add a 3-inch (7.5 cm) allowance on all sides. Cut a piece of fabric to this size.

2 Center the fabric over the desk-top, then smooth the edges over the top and over the edges. Staple the fabric to the underside of the top. Use enough staples to hold the fabric evenly and securely in place. You can minimize the number of wrinkles if you start by stapling the center of one long side, then the center of the oppo-site long side. Then work your way out toward the ends, smoothing the fabric as you go. Next, staple the cen-ter of each of the ends, and again work your way out toward the corners. Ease the fabric over the corners, elim-inating as many wrinkles as possible.

3 To protect the desktop, we rec-ommend placing a piece of clear plastic sheeting or glass over the com-pleted desktop.

EASY FABRIC-COVERED SHELF

This fabric-covered shelf requires only five pieces of wood and a small investment of time to complete. It's a terrific place to showcase a special collection or grouping of photographs.

MATERIALS

15 linear feet (4.5 m) of 1 x 6 pine

Wood glue

1⅝-inch (4 cm) nails, approximately 15 to 20

1 piece of fabric measuring 16½ by 70 inches (42 x 175 cm)

TOOLS

Scissors

Hammer

Staple gun and staples

INSTRUCTIONS

Making the Shelf

1 Cut a 52-inch (1.3 m) length from 1 x 6 pine. This will be the top of the shelf.

2 Cut two side pieces from the boards, each measuring 52 inches (1.3 m) long.

3 Place the two sides parallel to each other, spacing them 4 inches (10 cm) apart. Position the top piece on the edges of the two sides, as shown in figure 1. Apply wood glue to the surfaces where the pieces meet. Using the hammer and the 1⅝-inch (4 m) nails, nail through the top into the edges of the sides. Continue nailing along the top, spacing the nails approximately 6 inches (15 cm) apart.

Figure 1

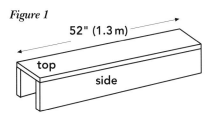

4 Cut two end pieces from the boards, each measuring 6¼ inches (15.6 cm) long.

5 Fit the end pieces over the top and sides, as shown in figure 2. Apply glue to the surfaces where the end pieces meet the top and sides. Using a hammer and the 1⅝-inch (4 cm) nails, nail through the edges of the ends into the sides and top. Use six nails on each end piece, spacing two nails on each of its three sides.

Figure 2

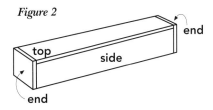

Covering the Shelf

1 Cut a piece of fabric measuring 16½ by 70 (42 x 175 cm) inches.

2 Center the fabric over the top of the shelf, then pull the edges of the fabric over the top edge of the shelf and over the sides. Staple the fab-

ric to the underside of the shelf. You can minimize the number of wrinkles if you first staple the center of one side, staple the center of the opposite side, then work your way out toward the corners. Smooth the fabric as you go. Staple the center of the remaining sides, and again work your way toward the corners. Be generous with the staples; use enough to keep the fabric from puckering along the sides. Tuck the corners in neatly and uniformly (right-angle "hospital" corners are ideal), then staple the fabric in place.

MATERIALS

Old lamp with cylindrical base

Old lampshade (either white or off-white)

½ yard (.45 m) of fabric for the base—we suggest a heavyweight fabric that will hold its shape

1 yard (.9 m) of fabric to cover the lampshade—we suggest a gauze-like, lightweight fabric with no body that will stretch and drape easily*

Scrabble tiles—it took approximately 70 tiles to trim our lampshade

Iron-on seam tape

TOOLS

Scissors

Iron and ironing board

Glue gun and glue sticks

Straight pins

This amount of fabric will cover a medium-sized lampshade—purchase more if your lampshade is larger

LAMP AND LAMPSHADE

We recycled an old lamp, then covered a plain lampshade to coordinate with our room. You can cover any lamp that has a cylindrical base using fabric to match your décor.

INSTRUCTIONS

Covering the Base

1 Measure the height of your lamp base. To that measurement, add 1 inch (2.5 m). Next, measure the circumference of your lamp base. To that measurement, add 1 inch (2.5 cm). Cut a piece of fabric to these dimensions.

2 Use iron-on seam tape to make a 1¾-inch (4.5 cm) hem in the top, bottom, and one side of the fabric piece.

3 Wrap the fabric around the base of the lamp, covering the unhemmed side with the hemmed side. Secure the fabric in place, using a glue gun.

Covering the Lampshade

1 Drape the fabric for the lampshade over the top of the shade, centering it so the entire lower edge of the shade is covered with fabric. Use straight pins to temporarily hold it in place.

2 Pull the fabric into gentle even gathers. When you are satisfied with the gathers, glue the fabric to the bottom edge of the shade. Cut off the excess fabric at the bottom of the shade and remove any straight pins.

3 From the fabric, cut around the circular top of the shade, leaving a ¼-inch (6 mm) allowance of fabric. Wrap the allowance to the inside top of the shade, and glue it in place, clipping the curves of the allowance where necessary.

4 Glue the tiles (letter-side-down) around the bottom edge of the finished shade to hide the raw edges of the fabric. It will look more interesting if you glue the tiles at varying heights.

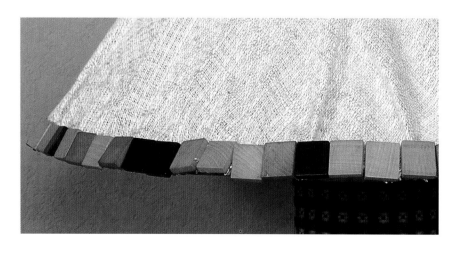

BLUE BEDROOM

Nothing transforms a room quicker than small decorative touches. The double-swagged window treatment is just lengths of fabric draped over a curtain rod. The bulletin board is an easy-to-make accessory that brightens any room, while providing a practical way to leave messages for busy family members. The footstool is just a few tucks and staples away from being done.

DOUBLE-SWAGGED DRAPE

Being quick and easy to make and hang, this swag will grace a window in no time. If you wish, you could use one color of fabric. However, we think using two colors opens many more possibilities for coordinating a room.

INSTRUCTIONS

Determining the Amount of Fabric

Most standard double windows require 10 yards (9.2 m) of fabric for a single swag. A good way to determine exactly how much fabric you need is use a length of rope to simulate the fabric, then swag the curtain rod with the rope as you would with fabric. Next, measure the rope used for the swag, add an extra yard (.9 m), and you have the correct measurement.

1 Attach the curtain rod and rod holders to the wall following the manufacturer's instructions.

2 Fold the two selvage edges right sides together in the center of the fabric to form a cylinder.

3 With the selvages on the side facing the wall, gather the cylinder across its width with your hands.

4 Place the gathered portion of the fabric over the rod until one end puddles nicely on the floor.

5 Pull the opposite end of the fabric over the rod, again gathering it with your hands, and placing it over the rod.

6 Repeat step 5 to create as many swags as you wish. Repeat steps 2 through 6 with the second fabric, following the swags of the first fabric.

7 Adjust the swags as necessary until they are all even. Pin the end of the swagged fabrics to hide the raw edges.

MATERIALS

Approximately 10 yards (9.2 m) each of two colors of 54-inch-wide (1.37 m) fabric

Curtain rod

Curtain rod holders

TOOLS

Scissors

Straight pins

Measuring Tape (optional)

BULLETIN BOARD

Replace your standard, boring, corkboard bulletin board with one that coordinates with your room. The gimp or ribbon provides a pin-less way to display postcards and messages.

INSTRUCTIONS

1 Cut the fabric to size.

2 Place the fabric wrong side down on a flat work surface. Place the quilt batting over the fabric, matching the edges. Center the plywood over the quilt batting.

3 Fold the fabric over the edges of the plywood and staple them in place. Use enough staples to hold the fabric evenly and securely in place. You can minimize the number of wrinkles if you start by stapling the center of one of the long sides, then the center of the opposite long side. Then work your way out toward the ends, smoothing the fabric as you go. Next, staple the center of each of the ends, and again work your way out toward the corners. Ease the fabric over the corners, eliminating as many wrinkles as possible.

4 Trim off the excess fabric and batting with scissors.

Adding the Gimp or Ribbon

1 Following the photo, weave the gimp or ribbon in position, then attach to the board. Staple the gimp or ribbon to the back side of the bulletin board, pull it across the front, and again staple it to the back side. Cut the gimp or ribbon on the backside, and repeat the procedure.

2 Staple each intersection of the gimp or ribbon.

3 Use hot glue to attach a button over the staple at each intersection.

4 Use the picture-frame hanging kit to hang the board on your wall.

MATERIALS

¾-inch (1.9 cm) plywood, one piece measuring 2 x 3 feet (61 x 91.5 cm)

Fabric in the color of your choice, one piece measuring 2½ x 3½ feet (76 x 106.5 cm)

Quilt batting, one piece measuring 2½ x 3½ feet (76 x 106.5 cm)

7 yards (6.4 m) of gimp or ribbon in a color that contrasts with your fabric

11 buttons in various colors— we purchased a pre-packaged assortment

Wire picture-frame hanging kit

TOOLS

Scissors

Measuring tape

Staple gun and staples

Glue gun and glue sticks

EASY STYLE ROOM BY ROOM 123

FOOTSTOOL

*Cover an ordinary footstool with fabric to match the other upholstery
in your room, and you've added a unique accessory to your décor. Use
it in front of a coordinated chair, or under a window or shelf to carry
the fabric around the room and add an extra touch of color.*

MATERIALS

Fabric in a color of your choice

TOOLS

Scissors
Staple gun and staples

INSTRUCTIONS

Determining the Amount of Fabric

To determine the amount you need, first
measure from the bottom of the front of
the stool, over the top, and to the bottom
of the back. Next, measure from the bottom of one side, over the top, and to the
bottom of the opposite side. Add a 2-inch
(5 cm) allowance on all four sides.

Covering the Footstool

1 Cut a piece of fabric to the proper
size.

2 Center the fabric over the footstool
bottom, and staple it to the underside.
You can minimize the number of wrinkles
if you first staple the center of one side,
then the center of the opposite side. Then
work your way out toward the corners.
Smooth the fabric as you go. Staple the
center of the remaining sides, and again
work your way toward the corners. Be generous with the staples; use enough to keep
the fabric from puckering along the sides.

3 Tuck the corners in neatly and uniformly (right-angle "hospital" corners
are ideal), then staple the fabric in place.

ACKNOWLEDGEMENTS

As is always the case, this book could not have been completed without the contributions of many people. We would like to give a standing ovation to the following...

Our extreme thanks to Waverly, a division of F. Schumacher, for providing all the fabrics, wallpaper, and borders for this book. We could not have produced such a beautiful book without their fabulous designs. All of their wonderful products can be seen on their web site. Just visit www.fschumacher.com and they will guide you through a very user-friendly search for all of their wallpaper, fabrics, and other products.

We are also indebted to Decra-Mold, Kay-Wood Industries for all of the beautiful and original moldings, ledges, and the faux fireplace used in the production of this book. You can contact them at: P.O. Box 75248, Oklahoma City, Oklahoma 73147; phone, 405-236-4661. Their fax is: 1-800-346-3963. Or your can visit their web site: www.decramold.com.

A huge thank you to Sherwin-Williams for providing the paint that brought all our projects together. You can reach them at The Sherwin-Williams Company, 101 Prospect Avenue N.W., Cleveland, Ohio 44115; or call 1-800-4-SHERWIN. To locate a store near you, check out their web site at www.sherwinwilliams.com.

Additional thanks to Wagner Spray Tech Corporation for providing power painting equipment. Their address is: Wagner Spray Tech Corporation, 1770 Fernbrook Lane, Minneapolis, Minnesota 55447.

At Lark Books, thanks to Jane LaFerla, our editor, who held our hands and transformed our sow's-ear manuscript into a silk purse in record time, and who did it all with humor and patience. To Chris Bryant, art director, who worked hours beyond the call to make certain that our photos are the best they can be, and who produced a beautiful book layout in record time.

Again, for the seventh time, a big thanks to Evan Bracken of Light Reflections, of Hendersonville, North Carolina, who created the wonderful photos and made the photo shoot a pleasurable experience.

A special thanks to Skip Wade who spent most of his vacation lending a hand in photo styling.

And to interior designers Diane Thompson and Nancie Shaw, both of Sarasota, Florida—thanks for your talent!

INDEX